THE BOOK OF REVELATION

A SERIES OF OUTLINE STUDIES IN THE

APOCALYPSE

By
JAMES H. McCONKEY

174th Thousand

SILVER PUBLISHING SOCIETY
BESSEMER BUILDING
PITTSBURGH, PA.

PASS IT ON

Here is a simple plan by which you can aid us in passing on this book to others. *Let us mail you free a* **lending copy**; *that is, a copy not to be retained but kept in circulation among your friends by* **lending**. Address the publishers.

Leaflet Messages by James H. McConkey

The Abundant Life
Beauty for Ashes
Believing is Seeing
The Blessed Hope
The Blessing of Doing
The Blood Covenant
Chastening
Committal
The Dedicated Life
Eternal Life
Faith
The Father's House
The Fifth Sparrow
Give God a Chance
God-Given Men
God's Jewel Case
The God-Planned Life
Guidance
Highway of Guidance
Holy Ground
If We Neglect
In and Out
Jacob's Struggle
Lame Feet
Law and Grace
A Message of Comfort
The Ministry of Suffering
The New Commandment
The Nutshell of Prophecy
Notes on Ephesians
Prayer
Prayer and Healing
Resurrection Victory
Safety
The Spirit-Filled Life
The Sure Shepherd
The Word

Book Messages by James H. McConkey

The Three-Fold Secret of the Holy Spirit
The Surrendered Life
The Way of Victory
The Book of Revelation
The End of the Age
Prayer

Sent free to any address
Supported by voluntary offerings

SILVER PUBLISHING SOCIETY
Bessemer Building
PITTSBURGH 22, PA., U. S. A.

CONTENTS

I.

INTRODUCTION

Introduction

"The Revelation of Jesus Christ which God gave unto Him to show unto His servants."—(Rev. 1:1)

Foreword

Note the title of the book. It is not "the concealment" but "the revelation" of Jesus Christ. It is well to mark this. For many say this book of Revelation is a mystery; it is a sealed book; God never meant nor expected His children to understand it. But the mere title of the book refutes such a view. For revelation means the "uncovering" or "unveiling" of that which has been hidden, not the concealing of it. Moreover, the next sentence declares that God gave it unto Jesus Christ *"to show unto His servants."* Hence we cannot defend our neglect and woeful ignorance of this wondrous book by asserting that it is not meant to be known. God says it *is,* and that it is *given* to *be shown,* not to be concealed. Neither does He tell us it is useless to read it. On the contrary He pronounces a special blessing upon the reading of it when He says (v. 3):

"Blessed is *he that readeth* and *they that hear* the words of this prophecy."

Salutation

Then follows the salutation. It is rich, precious, and beautiful. It strikes at the outset the dominant note of the book. It is the note of *Christ and His Coming.* Jesus Christ the faithful witness; the first-begotten from the dead; the Prince of all earth's kings; the one who loved, washed, and lifted us into kingship and eternal priesthood—this Christ is coming again! And every eye shall see Him, even those who pierced Him. And then—the shadowed background of that coming for those who know Him not—"all kindreds of the earth shall wail because of Him." And now John gives the setting of his story. He was in the isle of Patmos. On the Lord's day he was "in the Spirit." He heard behind him a great voice as of a trumpet. He turns and beholds seven golden candlesticks. These candlesticks are declared (v. 20) to be "the seven churches." In the midst of these he beholds the first great vision of the Revelation. It is the picture of

The Christ of the Revelation

Our thoughts go back naturally to the Christ who came to earth. We think of His helpless babehood; His beautiful and obedient childhood; His obscure young manhood; His life, His humiliation, His sufferings; His shameful death at the hands of wicked men.

And it is well that our memory should dwell much upon the Christ who lived and walked, the Son of Man, upon this earth. But this scene in Revelation is the picture of the Christ of today. It is the Christ who sits at the right hand of God in the glory. This is the coming Christ. This is the Christ whom we should think of as we wait and look for His coming. And what a figure! The Spirit ransacks the realm of nature for symbols that might convey some faint conception to our dull and finite human minds of the glory, splendor, and majesty of this coming One, who is the Christ of Revelation. His voice is as the roar of a thousand rushing rivers. His countenance is as the unbearable vision of the mid-day sun. His feet shine as the white light of brass in a seven-times heated furnace. His eyes are as flaming fire. John, the very John who had leaned upon the bosom of Christ upon earth, "fell at His feet as dead" when he caught the vision of this glorified Christ who is to come back to earth. All the way through this book of Revelation this Christ whom we meet is a Christ of kingship, majesty, power, and ineffable glory.

And now, at the word of His glorified Lord, John writes the first great message of the Book. It is the mesage to

The Churches of the Revelation

Let us note concerning these seven churches, that

These churches all existed at the time of the Revelation. The Spirit gives us the list of them in Chap. 1:11, as follows:

Ephesus
Smyrna
Pergamos
Thyatira
Sardis
Philadelphia
Laodicea

The names of some of these churches are more familiar to us than others. But evidently they all existed in John's time. And to each one of them is sent a very definite, personal message from the Lord Himself, for

The All-Seeing Christ stands in the midst of these churches.

"In the midst of the seven candlesticks one like unto the Son of man" (1:13).

That was what John saw when he turned at the sound of the voice. The scene shows Christ in the midst of His churches. It pictures Him "with eyes as a flame of fire" intensely scrutinizing them. His gaze pierces through and through. All things are open before Him. Nothing can be hid from such eyes as His. He sees their faults, failures, lukewarmness, wanderings, coldness, and indifference. He sees too all of their graces, goodness, and fidelity to Him and His commands. And here, after searching them to their innermost being, He pronounces His verdict upon them. Note that—

His message is one of joint rebuke and commendation. All the way through these churches Christ's message is one of mingled rebuke and praise. He finds in them both shortcomings and overcomings. Note them in order—

The Shortcomers

Ephesus—left her first love (2:4).
Smyrna—plagued with hypocrites (2:9).
Pergamos—holders of false doctrine (2:14-15).
Thyatira—suffering corrupt teachers (20:20).
Sardis—spiritual deadness (3:1).
Philadelphia—a little strength (3:8).
Laodicea—spiritual lukewarmness (3:16).

To all these churches He has an explicit message of rebuke, except, perhaps, to Philadelphia. And even with her the "faint praise" of 'a little strength" has in it too the shadow of rebuke. But mark too His beautiful spirit of commendation for all who overcome in His church.

The Overcomers

Ephesus—they shall eat of the tree of life (2:7).
Smyrna—they shall not be hurt of the second death (2:11).
Pergamos—they shall eat of the hidden manna (2:17).
Thyatira—they shall rule the nations (2:26).

Sardis—they shall be clothed in white raiment
3:5).

Philadelphia—they shall be pillars in God's temple
(3:12).

Laodicea—they shall sit with Christ on His throne
(3:21).

Again—

These churches are evidently a type of the whole Church of Christ. The very *number* of the churches hints at this. Seven is one of the most frequent typical numbers of the Scripture. It signifies perfection, fulness, completeness. It therefore suggests on its surface that these churches symbolize the entire church of Christ. Then, too, mark the *space* given to them. This book of Revelation is so terse and condensed that but one chapter is given to the Millennium, and less than one to the Advent of Christ. That these two chapters here, comprising ten per cent of the book, should be given over to messages to the seven churches bespeaks the wider scope of the messages.

Moreover the Revelation is declared (1:1) to be to all the "servants" of God, therefore this message to the churches seems to have this wider sweep of the church at large, rather than that of these seven churches only. Some think this to be

A chronological picture. They see in Ephesus who had "left her first love" the history of the declension of the apostolic church the first few centuries after her Lord had departed from them. Then in each successive church of the seven they trace the record of the church on earth as in exact correspondence. That history culminates in Laodicea with its lukewarmness and apostacy, as the last of the series. There is much that is interesting and striking in this theory of the seven churches. There are also some difficulties. Others see

A composite picture. The photographer may today take the photographs of seven faces and combine them into one which he calls a composite photograph, reproducing the traits of the entire seven. So, say some, the church of today is a composite picture of these seven churches of the Revelation. The church of today, they say, and of every age in the past, has the salient features of the seven. For in every church age we may find many who have left their first love, many spiritually dead, many carried away by false doctrine, many lukewarm ones, and so on through the whole seven-fold picture of the Revelation churches. It is indeed striking and interesting to run through the list and note how true this is. In the chronologic, and the composite pictures we have then the two principal views of the seven churches as types of the whole Church of Christ.

* * *

The Prelude to the Revelation

(Chaps. 4 and 5)

"The Revelation of Jesus Christ, which God *gave unto* Him *to show unto* His servants . . . and He sent and *signified* it . . . unto His servant **John** (1:1).

We here quote, in part, the very first words of the Revelation. They are an exact, concise statement of its scope and purpose. They state simply and clearly that God was the author of the Revelation; that He *gave* it to Jesus Christ; that Jesus Christ was to open or *show* it unto us, God's servants; and that He was to do this through John, His servant. Now the fourth and fifth chapters are a simple unfolding of the first verse of the book, which verse is indeed a perfect outline of the chapters. For in them we see first,

God upon the throne as *the Author* of the Revelation

"And One sat upon the throne" (Chap. 4:5).

God holds in His hand the sealed Book of the future

"And I saw in the right hand of Him that sat on the throne *a Book,* sealed with seven seals" (5:1).

God *gives* this book to Jesus Christ

"And He (Christ) came and *took the Book*" (5:7).

Jesus Christ *opens* this Book of Revelation of the future

"And I saw when *the Lamb opened* one of the seals" (6:1).

Jesus Christ *signifies* this message to us *by John.*

These two chapters thus simply expand and amplify the first verse of Revelation. They are clearly introductory. They are simply the prelude to the impending opening of the Sealed Book by Jesus Christ. They are the majestic avenue up which the mind of the reader travels until he stands before the Christ-opened portals of the Seals.

* * *

The Heart of the Revelation

We now reach the Sealed Book of the sixth and seventh chapters. Many say this Sealed Book stands for the title-deeds of the inheritance which belongs to Christ and which He is soon to assume. But let us pause a moment and ask ourselves a question. What is the symbolism of a seal? A seal may indeed be used to attest the signature to a title-deed. But it is also used *to conceal and safeguard the contents of a written document.* We seal a letter for that purpose. In prophecy God uses the seal in precisely this way. He tells Daniel (Dan. 12:4) concerning certain prophecies which are to be hidden that he is to "seal the book." He tells John concerning the very prophecies of this book of Revelation which He wants disclosed to His servants "seal not the sayings of the prophecy of this book" (Rev. 22:10). This use of the seal, therefore, to conceal the prophetic word seems to be the clear and natural usage here with the seven-sealed book rather than to give to the seals the meaning of an attestation to Christ's title-deeds. Proof positive seems to be found in the added fact that when the sealed book is opened there is not a trace of a title-deed seen or described therein. On the other hand as these seals are broken a series of stupendous and major prophetic events is unrolled by the seal-breaking hand of the Christ who is the Revealer of all the prophecies of this book. We are led to believe, therefore, as we shall presently see more fully, that this seven-sealed book cannot be subordinated to the place of a mere title-deed. Its place is more vital—

It is the very heart of the Revelation of Jesus Christ. It is the dramatic centre of its complex action. It is the story-thread of its wondrous narrative. It is the frame-work upon which the whole structure of the book is built. In it the scroll of New Testament prophecy is unrolled by Jesus Christ Himself as He breaks these seals in their divinely appointed order.

II.

THE STORY-THREAD or A. B. C.

The A. B. C. or Story-Thread of Matthew Twenty-four

And now we ask ourselves three important questions. The first is—

What is the Theme of the Revelation?

It stands forth sharply and clearly to the attentive reader. Here is the theme of the Revelation in a nut-shell. *The book has to do pre-eminently with the End of this present Age, and with the Coming again of Jesus Christ as the supreme and tremendous climax of the Age.* This is the great theme which is unrolled by the sublime and swift-moving panorama of events which make up the warp and woof of this wonderful book.

The second question is—

Does the Book of Revelation have an A. B. C. or Story-Thread?

We say *story-thread.* For with most of us here is the difficulty with the Book of Revelation. We cannot discern *its story-flow.* It is like a maze without a clue; it is a rich tapestry whose intricate pattern we cannot decipher. It seems a mass of figures, metaphors, and strange symbols. If we could only catch *the thread of its story* then the book would begin to clear up to us. Is there such a thread? Is there such a simple story-flow running through the book as will enable us to really grasp and understand its wonders? We believe there is. Moreover, we believe it to be so simple and, when once grasped, so clear that the reader may master and know the book with such a measure of completeness and satisfaction as shall transform his vision of it.

Did Christ ever tell this Revelation Story before?

This is a most vital question. For if Christ ever told this story before, especially in briefer form, it would naturally furnish us the Story-Thread to this later and more complicated story of the Revelation which we are here studying. Now Jesus Christ did tell before this very same story of the End of the Age and of His Coming again. And He told it to His same servant John. For on the Mount of Olives years before Christ sat and told to John and three other disciples the same story, in great brevity and simplicity, which He told in all its fulness and richness years later to John alone upon the isle of Patmos.

Here, then, is an open secret. The Olivet story of Christ's Second Advent is the clue to the Book of Revelation. It is in a nut-shell what the Revelation is in full. It is the Master's pencil-sketch of which Revelation is the complete painting.

The key to the story which Christ tells

from heaven is this story which Christ
told on earth years before. The twenty-
fourth chapter of Matthew is the seed of
New Testament prophecy, of which Revelation is the full-blown flower.

Let us turn therefore to—

The A. B. C. or Story-Thread of Matthew Twenty-four

You remember the story. His disciples had been showing Him the great temple. They had pointed out to Him its lofty pinnacles, its rich adornments, its massive stones. And then the Lord turns to them and quietly says: "There shall not be left here one stone upon another, that shall not be thrown down." Doubtless they were amazed, and perplexed. I can fancy them saying one to another, "Tomorrow we will go up to the Mount of Olives with Him. There we will sit at His feet and hold sweet communion as is our wont. Let us ask Him then what He means by this strange remark." So when they had come to the Mount and the Master was seated, they say,

"Tell us when shall these things be?

"And what shall be the sign of Thy coming and of the end of the age?"

The Double Question

Note that they asked of Him a double question. There is a line of cleavage between the first clause and the second. First, *"When*

---

*This chapter is reprinted in part from the author's book, "The End of the Age," which will be sent free to any one addressing the publishers of this book.

shall these things be?" And by "these things"
they meant the downfall of Jerusalem, and
the overthrow of the temple of which He had
just spoken, a disaster which was to take
place in less than a half century from that
time. Second, they asked Him, *"What shall
be the sign of Thy coming, and of the End
of the Age?"* a dual event which has not yet
taken place, and which is separated from the
first named catastrophe by almost two thousand years of time. Thus His answer covers
events separated by a gap of many centuries
simply because their question refers to both.
The same line of cleavage in the disciples'
interrogation appears therefore in Christ's
answer. It cuts that answer sharply in twain
between the fourteenth and fifteenth verses
of this chapter. The first fourteen verses
have to do with the first clause of their in-
quiry, "When shall these things be?" The
remainder of the chapter is His reply to the
second clause, "What shall be the sign of thy
coming and of the end of the age?" Let us
now note that He answers by giving

a. *The general Signs of the Whole Age.*

b. *The Special Signs of the End of the Age.*
Note that He gives the general signs of the
whole age in the sixth and seventh verses as
follows:

6 And ye shall hear of *wars and rumors of wars;*
see that ye be not troubled; for all these things must
come to pass, *but the end is not yet.*

7 For nation shall rise against nation, and kingdom

against kingdom: and there shall be *famines, and pestilences, and earthquakes,* in divers places.

Wars
Famines
Pestilence
Earthquakes.

Mark that of these He distinctly says (v. 6), "the end is *not yet.*" That is, these are the general marks of the whole age, but they are not the marks of *the end* of the age. There must be some *special* sign which marks that end in addition to these general signs which mark the whole age. So He passes on to give these special signs of the age-end. The first of these He names in verse twenty-one:

"When ye (v. 15) therefore shall see THE ABOMINA-TION OF DESOLATION *spoken of by Daniel the Prophet, stand in the holy place (whoso readeth let him under-stand), then let them which be in Judaea flee unto the mountains . . . for then shall be* GREAT TRIBU-LATION" (v. 21).

He puts His finger on one supreme, vital fact which foreruns and determines the end.

"When ye shall see The Abomination of Desolation"

That is the mysterious phrase with which He brings us face to face with the pivotal-point of the end. What does He mean? He cites it as though it were to them a familiar fact. He says it was "spoken of by Daniel the prophet." Let us follow the clue He indi-cates.

If we turn to the last chapter of the prophecy named (Daniel 12:11), we will note the interesting fact that centuries before Daniel had asked of the Lord the same question the disciples had just put to Christ. God had been revealing to him the startling events of the end-time. As He unrolled the page of all future history to His devoted servant and the solemn and awe-inspiring procession of coming events moved across the stage before Daniel's astonished gaze his soul was awed and astounded within him and he cried out in wonder, *"O my Lord, what shall be* THE END *of these things?"* And then God places His finger upon this same strange figure to which Christ has referred and says to Daniel that *"From the time that . . . the Abomination that maketh desolate is set up,"* until the end shall be a certain period of somewhat over three and a half years.

Thus when Daniel asks as to the end God points him to an ominous figure called Abomination of Desolation and tells Daniel that this portentous personage marks the end-time. When His apostles ask as to the end Jesus Christ puts His finger upon this very same mark and tells them that when they see "The Abomination of Desolation spoken of by Daniel the prophet" then the fierce crisis of all history is upon them. So, whether this mark is an individual person or, as some think, an image of the same set up in the temple, matters not for our purpose.

Either himself or the image of him as suddenly revealed in the temple constitutes the crucial mark of the age-end so near at hand, yea, even then begun.

Is there anything else in the New Testament which tells us that some portentous personage must appear before the time when God appears in the glory of His manifestation? Assuredly there is. For Paul when speaking of this very glorious appearing of the Lord Jesus Christ says exactly the same thing. He declares explicitly that before that great event there must be revealed another personage, even as Daniel and Christ have already stated before him. "For

"That day shall not come except *that Man of Sin be revealed,* the *Son of Perdition;* who *opposeth* and exalteth himself above all that is called God, or that is worshipped; so that he as God sitteth in the temple of God, shewing himself that he is God" (2 Thess. 2:3-4).

As the crucial sign of the age-end there is to appear in this world a sinful MAN. So colossal is his wickedness that he is called "The Man of Sin" (v. 3). He is called too "The Son of Perdition," a name of perfidy applied to only one other man in the New Testament—Judas Iscariot (v. 3). He opposes God, and exalts himself above all gods, both the true and the false (v. 4). He bears rule over the entire world in his coming day (Rev. 13). His full-length portrait is painted in all its hideousness in Rev. 13. He is

The Abomination of Desolation of Daniel; the same of Christ as mentioned here; the Man of Sin of Paul; and the Anti-Christ of John.

With the Anti-Christ is coupled a GREAT TRIBULATION. When he is manifested this Tribulation breaks forth—a Tribulation such as the world has never seen before. The words of Christ are clear upon this—Matt. 24:21:

"Then shall be great tribulation such as was not since the beginning of the world to this time, no, nor ever shall be."

* * * *

God's Range Lights

Have you ever seen a pair of what the sailors call "range lights"? And have you ever watched them in action? You are taking a voyage by ocean or lake. Presently you approach your destination. As the harbor looms up in the distance the pilot calls your attention to the various lights along the shore. Most of them seem scattered and unrelated. But, by and by, two lights flash out which seem to be close and coming into line. The wheelsman informs you these are "range lights." He tells you to watch them coming into alignment with each other. Steadily you gaze at the brilliant lights. As you watch you note that the angle-gap between them is rapidly narrowing. Closer and closer they come. Now they are almost in line. An instant and they range to a hair's breadth with each other. Instantly the pilot swings his wheel swiftly to port or starboard. The tiller chains rattle and creak. The course is instantly changed into perfect alignment with the range lights. The great ship heads into port in unswerving conformity to the course set by the gleaming lights. They are the last lights of the voyage. When they loom up the journey's end is near.

So is it with such general signs of the age as War, Famine and Pestilence. They are red-lights scattered along the shores of *all* the centuries. They have no special significance. "The end is *not yet.*" But by and by shall loom up the twin danger lights of the Anti-Christ and Tribulation. They are God's great range-lights. When one is manifested the other also appears. "*When* ye shall see the Abomination of Desolation . . . *then* shall be great Tribulation." When they suddenly and swiftly come into alignment then this present age is nearing its voyage-end. "Then cometh the end."

This special sign is the beginning therefore of the real Story-Thread of the Age-End in Matthew 24. Here begins the A. B. C. of the Age-End story as follows:

A. The Anti-Christ and Tribulation

*   *   *   *

And now when the tribulation is ended what is the sign which follows? The Word of God is very clear here—

"Immediately after the tribulation of these days shall the sun be darkened, and the moon shall not give her light . . . ."

The sequence of the signs is clear. *"Immediately after the tribulation"* follows the second sign, namely—the sign in the Sun and Moon, or—

B. The Heavenly Sign

*   *   *   *

God veils the sun and moon in that strange, shadowing semi-gloom that makes the total eclipse fill men's hearts with solemn awe. This is the second sign. Not set up in the temple of Judæa, localized to the land as is the Abomination of Desolation, but hung out in the over-arching heavens where every eye upon earth can see it. The prophet Joel plainly speaks of this same sign and puts it where Christ does, *before* the final sign of the Son of Man, when he says (Joel 2:30-31)

"And I will show wonders in the heavens and in the earth, blood, and fire and pillars of smoke; the sun shall be turned into darkness, and the moon into blood,, *before* the great and the terrible day of the Lord shall come."

This portentous and awe-inspiring sign in mid-heaven warns them that are wise that but one more sign is left till the end. It quickly follows. What is it? Verse 30 of our chapter answers—

"*Then* (that is after the celestial signs) shall appear the sign of the Son of Man in Heaven," or—

C. The Second Advent of Christ

*   *   *   *

After the sign in the heavens "Then shall appear the sign of the Son of Man in Heaven." The verse may have a double construction. It may mean that the Son of Man is Himself the last sign. Or it may be quite possible that there is a sign of the Son of Man immediately before He Himself breaks from the heavens in dazzling glory. Shall there be such a sign? Shall the same star that blazed in portentous splendor over the hills of Bethlehem break forth in sudden glory again? Shall the glory of God suddenly fill the heavens as it filled them before the amazed vision of the trembling shepherds? Shall the awful symbol of His love and suffering which reared its blood-stained silhouette upon the dark hill of Calvary now shine forth for one unspeakable moment upon the gaze alike of men who have rejected the cross of Christ and those to whom it is the most precious symbol the world possesses? We know not. But whether the verse means that there shall be such a precedent sign, or whether not, certainly it is but a near, **swift and** splendid fore-runner of Himself, who **now** breaks forth from within the veil **and ap-** pears "apart from sin unto salvation." This is indeed the last sign. Here the age ends. Here shall begin the new one, the golden **one** of which men have sung, and dreamed, **and** written, but which no man shall see until they see Him who shall inaugurate its **glories** and wield the sceptre of its kingship.

* * * *

Notice how clearly and distinctly the **order** of these signs and events is seen by simply arranging the verses in their natural succession, as follows:

(v. 15)

"WHEN ye shall see the Abomination of Desolation," etc.

(v. 21)

"THEN shall be great Tribulation," etc.

(v. 29)

"IMMEDIATELY AFTER THE TRIBU-LATION of those days shall the sun be dark-ened," etc.

(v. 30)

"And THEN (the "then" of succession) *shall appear the sign of the Son of Man in heaven,"* etc.

Here then is the Story-Thread of Matthew 24 in its simplicity. Here is its A. B. C. in natural, logical order—

A. Anti-Christ and Tribulation

B. Heavenly Signs

C. Second Advent

The A. B. C. or Story-Thread of
THE SEALS

We have seen then the Story-Thread of Matthew Twenty-Four as to the end of this present age. In it Christ gives

First, the general signs of the whole age.
Second, the special signs of the end of the age.

And now as we approach the special study of the Book of Revelation we are confronted with this striking fact—

The A. B. C. or Story-Thread of the Seals of Revelation is exactly the same as this Story-Thread of Matthew Twenty-four.

Let us notice first Christ's statement of *the general marks of the whole age.* Three of the most striking of these are given in the sixth and seventh verses of that twenty-fourth chapter of Matthew. They are as follows—

"And ye shall hear of *wars and rumors of wars*" for *nation shall rise against nation* and *kingdom against kingdom* and there shall be *famines* and *pestilences* and earthquakes in divers places."

War, famine, and pestilence, are three of the notable signs of the whole age designated by Christ. Elsewhere He mentions the Gospel, which they are to preach throughout the age with the promise that He will be with

them till "the end of the age." There is no
time succession in these signs. They are
linked together as common marks of all the
centuries between the first and second coming of Jesus Christ. Jotting them down in
line we have then as four prominent marks
of this age—

    The Gospel
    War
    Famine
    Pestilence

Turn now to the sixth chapter of Revelation. Here Christ is pictured opening the
seven seals of the book. We read in the first
two verses—

*"And I saw when the Lamb opened one (the first)
of the seals . . . and behold a white horse; and he
that sat on him had a bow; and a crown was given
unto him; and he went forth conquering and to conquer."*

Turning to Rev. 19:11-12 we see there
Christ as He comes forth from heaven is a
crowned one and is seated upon a white
horse. The most reasonable interpretation
of this first seal would seem therefore to asso-
ciate it with *the Gospel* of Christ going forth
conquering and to conquer. This it has been
doing throughout all the centuries since our
Lord left His disciples' command to go forth
into the world and preach it till He came
again.

Coming now to *the second seal* we read
(vs. 3-4)—

And when he had opened the SECOND SEAL *there went out another horse that was* RED; *and power was given to him that sat thereon to* TAKE PEACE FROM THE EARTH, *and that they should* KILL ONE ANOTHER; *and there was given unto him a* GREAT SWORD.

Here is a plain picture of *War;* exactly the same as that mentioned next in Matt. 24:7 as cited above.

We read on (vs. 5-6)—

"And when he had opened the THIRD SEAL, *lo, a* BLACK HORSE *and he that sat on him had a pair of balances in his hand. And I heard a voice say, A measure of wheat for a penny, and three measures of barley for a penny."*

This with its picture of food so scarce as to be weighed in balances, and grain sold for a great price, is a clear picture of FAMINE, as all students agree. And Famine is linked with War in the Matthew passage already quoted.

And now in vs. 7 and 8 we read

"And when he had opened THE FOURTH SEAL *I looked and behold* A PALE HORSE; *and his name that sat on him was* DEATH."

The fourth seal is Death, and it practically corresponds with the last mentioned sign of Pestilence in Matthew 24, for pestilence is but one form of death, and later in this verse the same word is translated "pestilence." Note then the remarkable parallelism between the Matthew passage and these first four seals as we set them in opposition, one to another.

Matthew 24	**Revelation (Seals)**
The Gospel	*The Gospel* (White Horse)
War	*War* (Red Horse)
Famine	*Famine* (Black Horse)
Pestilence (Death)	*Death* (Pale Horse)

The resemblance here is striking. It seems to plainly show that the Mount of Olives story and the Revelation story are the same. But we need not remain in doubt. For we have a clear and simple test. Recall that Christ in his Olivet discourse first gives the above as the *general* signs of the age. Then He follows with the *special* signs of *the end* of the age. And the first of these age-end signs is, as we have seen, a Great Tribulation under the Anti-Christ. Now if the Revelation story is a parallel to the Matthew story then the first seal which follows these general signs above, namely, the Fifth, should disclose the first *special* sign of the *age-end*, namely, the Tribulation. And so it does. For "When he opened *the Fifth seal*" (Rev. 6:9-11), John saw under the altar the souls of those who had been martyred for the cause of God. They cry out to be avenged. They are told to *"rest yet for a little season until their fellow servants also and their brethren, that should be killed as they were, should be fulfilled."*

Teachers agree that this is a picture of the tribulation. For it represents those who have been martyred in by-gone centuries waiting for a little time until those who should suffer a like fate in the tribulation should have fulfilled their destined end. Thus the first sign of the end, in Matthew, is *Tribulation.* And the Fifth seal in Revelation is *Tribulation.*

And now the next link in this chain of proof is still stronger. You will recall our Lord saying again (Matt. 24:29) —

"Immediately after the tribulation of those days shall the sun be darkened and the moon shall not give her light."* The first sign was the Tribulation, under the Anti-Christ. The second sign is clear. It follows *"immediately after the tribulation."* It is the heavenly sign of darkened sun and moon. Now note this. If the Fifth seal *is* the Tribulation then the Sixth seal which follows it in time-order must be this heavenly sign in the sun and moon. And so it is. For note the word of the Book at this point (Rev. 6:12):

"And I beheld when he had opened THE SIXTH seal, and lo the SUN BECAME AS SACK-CLOTH OF HAIR, AND THE MOON BECAME AS BLOOD."*

Thus the order of the first and second signs of the age-end in Matt. 24, and the order of the Fifth and Sixth Seals in Revelation is precisely the same, being in both cases that of the Tribulation, then the Signs in the Sun and Moon.

What now is the third and last sign in the Matthew story? It is the sign of His own Coming by which the age is ended. (Matt. 24:30).

"*And then* (i. e., after the signs in sun and moon) *shall appear* THE SIGN OF THE SON OF MAN IN HEAVEN *and they shall see* THE SON OF MAN COMING."

But in the nineteenth chapter of Revelation (vs. 11-16) we see this Coming of the Son of Man in glory, as the chief event and climax of the Seventh Seal of Revelation under which it occurs. Thus the parallelism between the Matthew story and the Revelation story is as complete as it is remarkable. Set opposite to each other those stories stand like this—

Matthew		The Seals
(General Signs)		(General Signs)
The Gospel	1	*The Gospel*
War	2	*War*
Famine	3	*Famine*
Pestilence (Death)	4	*Death* (Pestilence)
(Special Signs)		(Special Signs)
TRIBULATION	5	TRIBULATION
SIGNS IN SUN		SIGNS IN SUN
AND MOON	6	AND MOON
ADVENT OF CHRIST	7	ADVENT OF CHRIST

Arranged by themselves in the form of a simple diagram the seven seals appear as follows:

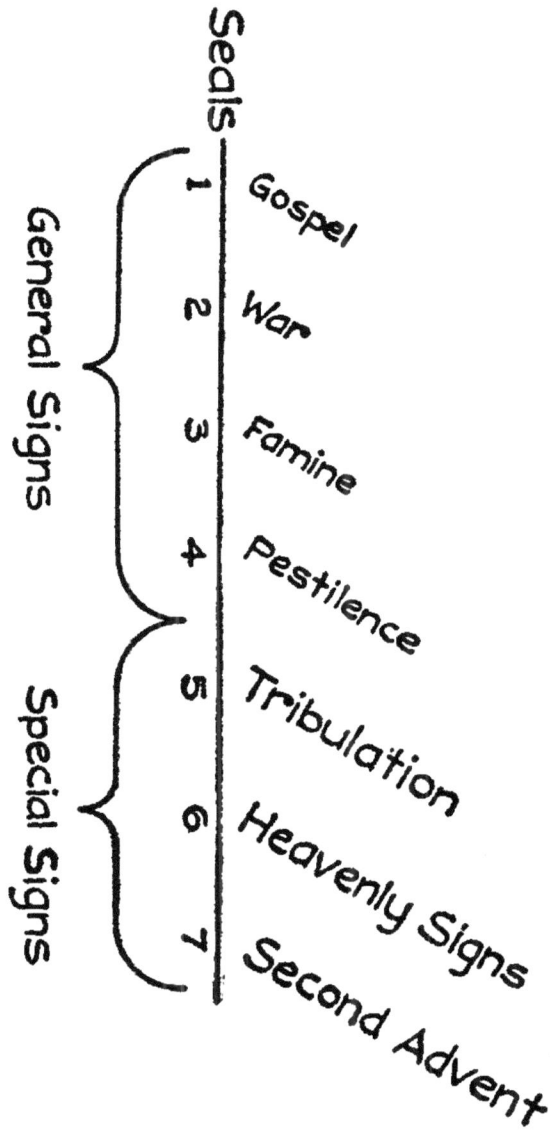

Thus the A. B. C. or Story-Thread of Matthew and that of the Seals of Revelation is exactly the same. Moreover, as we have already seen in the Matthew story it is not the general signs of the whole age but the special signs of the end of the age which constitute the A. B. C. of this age-end story. These signs as noted are The Tribulation, The Heavenly Signs, The Second Advent. So here in Revelation it is not the first four seals but the last three which are vital to the age-end story and carry its A. B. C. That A. B. C., as we have just seen, is exactly the same as in Matthew, as follows:

A.   (Fifth Seal)—TRIBULATION.

B.   (Sixth Seal)—HEAVENLY SIGNS.

C.   (Seventh Seal)—SECOND ADVENT.

THE SEALS
(Continued)

This exact identity of the Story-Thread of Matthew 24 and the Seals of Revelation is profoundly significant. What does it mean? There can be but one explanation—

These two stories are the same. For both tell of the same event, the coming again of Christ at the end of the age. The first was told on earth; the second from heaven. The first on the Mount of Olives; the second on lonely Patmos. The first to Peter, James, John and Andrew. the second to John alone. The first by Christ in the flesh; the second by Christ in the glory. Logically then they must agree, because they are the story of the same event. Scripturally they do agree and with the most marvelous precision, as we have seen. The Olivet story and the seven Seals are the clue to the Book of Revelation. They are the story-thread of which the book is the story-web. They are the Master's sketch of which the book is the complete painting. The Seals and the Olivet story unlock the Apocalypse.

*   *   *   *

But some one may wonder how these seals could occupy a place of such importance as we have ascribed to them since they seem to be almost confined to the sixth chapter in which six out of the seven are described. The answer to this brings us to one of the most vital and significant facts in this whole matter, namely, that

The whole structure of the Book of Revelation is built upon the frame-work of these Seven Seals.

As the first six seals move along in order each presents a distinct and complete picture in itself, ending with the Tribulation under the Fifth Seal, and the Heavenly Signs under the Sixth. But when we reach the Seventh Seal the action grows more intricate. Note the text of this seal (Chap. 8:1-2)—

1 And when he had opened the seventh seal, there was silence in heaven about the space of half an hour.

2 And I saw the seven angels which stood before God; and to them were given seven trumpets.

When this Seventh Seal is opened instead of presenting a single complete picture it develops or expands into Seven Trumpets, under which God pours forth a series of *Judgments* upon the earth. Now note the place and order of these Trumpets in relation to the Seventh Seal. It is not that the Seventh Seal ends and the Trumpets then begin. Quite the contrary. The Seventh develops into, or flowers out into these Seven

Trumpets. That is, the Trumpets are divisions, or sub-heads, as it were, of the Seventh Seal. They are details of that Seal and, in time and place, they come under that Seal. The Seven Trumpets do not *succeed the Seventh Seal*; they *compose it*. A simple diagram will illustrate this—

SEALS—1 2 3 4 5 6 7......................

TRUMPETS—1 2 3 4 5 6 7

Note that the Trumpets come *under* the Seventh Seal. And thus that Seal, as indicated by the dotted line, runs out over all the Trumpets, and includes them all. Thus, as has been said, the Seven Trumpets do not *follow* the Seventh Seal; they *form* it. Hence the Seventh Seal does not end with chapter eight. It covers both chapters eight and nine, which record the Trumpets.

Running hastily over these six trumpets in chapters eight and nine let the reader turn to chapter eleven, fifteenth verse, and note there the sounding of the Seventh Trumpet. As it is sounded the Elders cry (v. 18) to God, *"Thy Wrath is Come."* That is, under the Seventh Trumpet there is poured forth upon the earth what is here called "The Wrath of God." But turning to chapter 15:1, where this Wrath is poured forth we read (v. 1):

"And I saw another sign in heaven great and marvelous, *seven angels* having the *seven last plagues;* for in them is filled up the *wrath of God* . . . And one of the four beasts (v. 7) gave unto the seven angels *seven golden vials* full of the *wrath of God.*"

That is, when the Wrath is about to be poured out under the Seventh Trumpet, John sees Seven Angels with Seven Golden Vials, which represent this Wrath even as the Seven Trumpets represented the Judgments of God. Thus as the Seventh Seal has under it the Seven Trumpets, so also the Seventh Trumpet includes the Seven Vials as parts or divisions of itself. A simple diagram again will show, as before, that these Vials do not follow the Seventh Trumpet but are included under it as parts or divisions of the same. Thus—

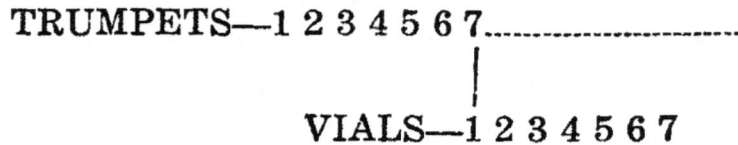

TRUMPETS—1 2 3 4 5 6 7........................
                                            |
                                            |
            VIALS—1 2 3 4 5 6 7

Here (as indicated by the dotted line) the Seventh Trumpet runs out over and includes all the Seven Vials. And now combining these two diagrams we obtain the full story-thread of the Seals in their inclusion of the trumpets and vials as follows:

SEALS—1 2 3 4 5 6 7 . . . .

TRUMPETS—1 2 3 4 5 6 7 . . . .

VIALS—1 2 3 4 5 6 7

SECOND ADVENT

* * * *

*The seventh seal—as indicated by the dotted lines—extends over all the trumpets. But the seventh trumpet extends over all the vials. Thus the seals include both all the trumpets and all the vials. And both seals, trumpets, and vials climax and end at one and the same great crisis-moment, the Second Advent of our Lord Jesus Christ. This diagram shows that the Seals are the heart of the Revelation, and that they form the framework of the entire book. Let the reader grasp it strongly and clearly and he has grasped the **A. B. C.** of the Book of Revelation.*

At first glance this diagram might seem complicated. As a matter of fact it is very simple. For let the reader recall the story-thread of the book as shown in the seals. There its A. B. C. is—

A. *Tribulation*
B. *Heavenly Signs*
C. *Second Advent*

Now the trumpets and vials add to this simple story two great ideas and two only. Under the seventh seal and before it ends, God pours forth upon the earth *Judgment* (under the trumpets) and *Wrath* (under the vials). That is we must add to the C. of the seventh seal these two ideas only and the A. B. C. of the seals expands simply and naturally into—

A. (Fifth Seal)—*Tribulation*

B. (Sixth Seal)—*Heavenly Signs*

C. (Seventh Seal)· Judgment (trumpets)

Wrath (vials)

Second Advent

The Climax of the Seals

(The Trumpets and Vials)

The Story-Thread climaxes, as we have just seen, in the Seventh Seal, which is the Advent seal. But this seal, as we have also just seen, adds to the story-thread the two dominant ideas of *Judgment,* under the trumpets, and *Wrath* under the vials. Let us consider these with a bit more of detail ere we leave them.

The Judgments (Trumpets)

(Read carefully Chapters 8, 9, and 11:15-19)
The Trumpets are periods rather than points of time. We think of them as points or instants of time. But they are evidently periods however brief. Thus the last trumpet which we think of as instantaneous covers, as has been seen, all the vials of wrath and must be at least a brief period. So, too, the locust-horde under the fifth trumpet scourge and torment men for five months (9:5), indicating that this trumpet must run for quite a period of time.

They increase in intensity as they progress. The first four fall upon the grass, trees, seas, and rivers; that is, upon the physical features of the earth. But the last three fall upon "men" (Chap. 9:3, etc.). This increase in intensity of the last three trumpets is shown in the cry of the angel in chapter 8:13.

"*Woe, woe, woe* to the inhabiters of the earth by reason of the other voices of the trumpet of the three angels."

This angelic cry has given to these last three trumpets the name of the Woe Trumpets. Thus the first woe is the fifth trumpet; the second woe is the sixth trumpet; and the third woe is the seventh or last trumpet.

Their symbols stand for realities. Many think because a thing is symbolic that it is unreal. And they thus interpret these trumpets. But nothing could be farther from the truth. A symbol is simply a concrete form of expressing a truth. When Christ speaks of the flames of hell this may seem to some to be a symbol. But if so it stands for an appalling reality. He simply uses that figure which will nearest express to our limited human understanding the tremendous fact which it expresses. So of the trumpets. There seems to be much of symbol and metaphor in their description. But it all stands for something tremendously real. And then too let the reader note this—

These trumpets will be understood perfectly when the time comes for their fulfilment.

Let it be remembered that this book of the Apocalypse will be God's last great word of revelation to the men of the age-end generation who are here upon the earth when Christ shall come again, and before whose astonished gaze all these things will pass in fulfilment, even as written. Then in the white light of this Revelation all things will be clearly understood. Therefore let not the reader perplex himself as to how far such things as the locust horde, and the two hundred million horsemen of these woe trumpets are literal or symbolic. Enough for us to know that they stand for *realities*, as already stated, and that they will be perfectly understood by the men of that age-end generation for whom God means them to be a great beacon-light illuminating the enveloping darkness as no word of man can do.

The Wrath (Vials)
(Chaps. 14 to 18)

The Prelude to the Wrath. Chapter 14 gives a series of pictures ere the Wrath of God is "filled up" in the vials. A hundred and forty-four thousand are seen who are called the "first-fruits" and are seemingly the same company as that seen in chapter 7. An angel flies through the heavens proclaiming an everlasting gospel and calling on men to fear God because the hour of His judgment is at hand (vs.6-7). Other angel heralds cry out concerning the fall of Babylon and the fate of those who worship the Beast (vs. 8-11). One like unto the Son of man reaps the harvest of the earth with His sickle (vs. 14-16). Another angel casts the grapes of the earth into the winepress of the wrath of God, which is seemingly the beginning of the wrath (vs. 18-20). And then the wrath is "filled up" (15:1) in *The Vials of Wrath* (Chaps. 15 and 16).

These picture the Wrath of God against Satan and Sin. Sometimes the tribulation is spoken of as the wrath of God. But it is rather the wrath of Satan. For he comes "having great wrath because he knoweth that he hath but a short time" (Rev. 12:12). The Jews are warned by Christ to flee from this wrath (Matt. 24:26). When it is ended then follows God's wrath as shown in these Vials. "For in these is filled up the wrath of God" (Chap. 15:1). It begins evidently with the Seventh Trumpet for when that is sounded the angel cries (11:15-18) *"Thy Wrath is come."* And then (Chap. 16), under this trumpet these Seven Vials fall in swift, intense wrath against Satan and the men who worship and give allegiance to him.

The Wrath Against Babylon (Chaps. 17-18)

In chapters 17 and 18 is pictured the wrath of God against Babylon. Babylon is evidently both a system and a city, just as Rome is both. The system represents apostate christendom at the age-end. The city is manifestly the great capital of the system. Seafaring men see its destruction afar off (18: 17). This apostate system has the ear-marks of Rome yet likely includes all of formal and nominal christendom. Typified by the Woman she sits upon seven mountains (17: 9); she is drunken with the blood of the saints (17:6) she traffics in "slaves and souls of men" (18:13), some of God's children dwell within her borders for a voice from heaven cries "come out of her, *my people*" (18:4) she has dominion over "nations and people" (17:15), hers is an ecclesiastical power and dominion as distinguished from that of the Beast she rides whose power is civil and political. She meets her doom at the hands of the Beast and his ten federated kings who "eat her flesh and burn her with fire" (17:16), they themselves being the instruments of God in this destruction, "For God hath put in their hearts to fulfil His will" (17:17). Thus the Woman is destroyed by the Beast, and in turn the Beast is destroyed by the Lord Jesus Christ at His Coming (19:20).

In the nineteenth chapter is the picture of the joy and gladness of the Marriage of the Lamb, following which comes the last stage of the Wrath in—

The Wrath at the Advent

(Chapter 19:11 to 21)

For let it be remembered that the Second Advent of Christ is an advent of judgment and wrath as to the unbelieving world. The tremendous picture in Revelation 19 of His coming forth from the heavens in majesty and glory is a picture of judgment for we are plainly told that

"In righteousness He doth judge and make war" (v. 11):

And the Spirit, through Paul depicting the same great scene (2 Thess. 1:7-8), says:

The Lord Jesus shall be revealed from heaven with His mighty angels, in flaming fire taking vengeance on them that know not God, and that obey not the gospel of our Lord Jesus Christ."

The man who eliminates justice and judgment from this concept of the Lord Jesus will find no comfort for his views in the Revelation picture of the Advent of Jesus Christ.

* * * *

The Story by Chapters

In reaching now the Second Advent of our Lord in the nineteenth chapter we arrive at the climax of the story-thread of the book of Revelation as we have been considering it. Let us note the chapters which have been covered in our study—

> *Introductory*—1 to 5.
> *The Seals*—6 and 8.
> *The Judgments*—8 to 11.
> *The Wrath*—15 to 18.
> *The Advent*—19.

About fifteen chapters out of the nineteen have been touched upon above in the story of the book as we have dealt with it. But

at least four have been omitted. And they
are four very important ones. What shall be
said of these? And where do they find their
place in the narrative? For the sake of clear-
ness and contrast with the main story-thread
we call these chapters—

The Insets

Here was a common sight in the days of
the great world-war. The artist of a great
illustrated paper depicts some graphic scene
of this colossal conflict. He fills a whole cover
page with his dramatic scene of charge,
struggle, or retreat. Then down in the cor-
ner of the picture he inserts a little circle or
square with the portrait of a notable figure,
with words beneath it *"The inset* is Foch."

Or the historian with his word-painting
may do the same thing as the artist with pen-
cil or brush. Here, for example, is some historian writing a history of our own war between the states. His story moves along in
perfect time-succession. He pictures one
great event after another through the months
and years. Then he suddenly pauses. Some
great personage appears upon the scene. He
is a central figure in the movement of the
story; a leader, statesman, or general. The
story of events would not be complete without a sketch of his striking and important
personality. So the historian pauses and in
a new chapter proceeds to give a sketch of

the birth, life, and characteristics of this important historical personage. Then he tells us that *the inset* is Lincoln, Lee, Grant, or Jackson. *This inset is not a time-unit of the story.* Rather the historian interrupts the time-flow of his story in order that he may depict it. Then he takes up again the real story-thread after he has finished the biographical inset.

This seems precisely the divine plan of the Book of Revelation. The seals, trumpets, and vials carry its story-flow. But the intervening chapters do not. They are not time-units of the story. They are episodes. They are like the biographical sketches which the historian pauses long enough in his main story to write. So these chapters are *the historical insets of the book.* They are sketches of great and important personages and characters which the Holy Spirit detaches from the main story-flow and pauses long enough to paint their portraits, after which he returns to the main thread of the story. When the reader clearly grasps the fact that each of these Revelation insets, however important, is still an inset, and is separate and detached from the main story-thread, confusion will at once vanish and each will take its own true and proper place, not as a time-unit, but as a parenthesis in the story. Let us now study these.

III.

THE INSETS

The Two Companies.
The Two Witnesses.
The Two Wonders.
The Two Beasts.

The Two Companies

(Chapter 7)

This chapter is an inset between the Tribulation which is the wrath of Satan, and The Seventh Seal, which ushers in the wrath of God. It pictures two great companies of individuals. They are here associated in the same place. Yet they are marked by sharp contrasts which will appear as we study them together.

* * * *

Their Place

The preceding chapter (the sixth) closes with the opening of the sixth seal (v. 12). Then is introduced this seventh chapter, with the inset of the Two Companies. This would seem to place them after the tribulation, since that comes under the fifth seal (v. 9). The context establishes this. For in this seventh chapter the answer to John's question as to the identity of the second company, is

"These are they which came out of great tribulation" (v. 14).

The tribulation is thus evidently past when these are seen. Then too concerning the first company of 144,000 the cry goes up (v. 3)

"Hurt not the earth, neither the sea, nor the trees, *till* we have sealed the servants of our God."

But the hurting of the earth, the trees, and the sea takes place in the following chapter

(8:7-8) by the judgments of God under the Seventh seal (8:1). Hence the sealing of this first company clearly takes place just before the Seventh seal. It is not, as some argue, to protect the 144,000 against the Tribulation. For that has already taken place under the fifth seal. It is to identify and secure them against these judgments of God which are about to fall upon earth, sea, and trees in the following chapter.

Between these two companies there are some marked contrasts. Let us note a few of them—

*   *   *   *

The first company is Jewish; the second, Gentile.

Verse 4 makes this perfectly clear—

"And there were sealed a hundred and forty and four thousand of all the tribes of *the children of Israel.*"

It is plain then that these are Jews. Who are they from among the Jewish people, and whence do they come? The same company evidently appears in chapter 14, where they are pictured as standing on Mount Sion with the Lamb (v. 1). And in verse 4 we read—

"These were redeemed from among men, being *the firstfruits* unto God and to the Lamb."

The Word of God is full of promises to the Jewish remnant when the Lord shall come again. Here, just before He appears, is seen a company which is called

"*Firstfruits* unto God and to the Lamb."

They are thus the first cluster of the harvest of Jews which God shall reap for Himself and Son in the days to come at the age-end. The second company, on the other hand, is Gentile. Verse 9 makes this clear—

"A great multitude . . . *of all nations, and kindreds and people, and tongues,* stood before the throne."

The word "gentiles" means "nations." Just as the first company is made up of Jews so is this second one composed of the nations of the world other than the Jews.

* * * *

The first company is numbered; the second, numberless.

The number of the first company is 144,-000. It is composed of 12,000 from each of the twelve tribes of the children of Israel (v. 4). If, as many think, this number is literal then we have here a suggestive glimpse of the wondrous system, and organization of Christ's Millennial reign over Israel. Recall that He said to His own disciples when on earth, and speaking of His coming kingdom

"Ye also shall sit upon twelve thrones, judging the twelve tribes of Israel" (Matt. 19:18).

The twelve are to be associated with Him in the rulership of the twelve tribes of Israel. Then out of these twelve tribes are chosen these twelve thousand each, of this first com-

pany in the seventh chapter of Revelation.
Their close association with Christ is shown
in the statement (14:4)

"These are they which follow the Lamb whither-
soever He goeth."

In this picture of His own as judges,
throne-mates, and associates we have a beautiful suggestion of the perfect order, system,
and harmony of His kingdom which is to
come.

The second company is *numberless.* For
in the ninth verse they are called—

"A great multitude *which no man could number.*"
We cannot but see here the close connection
between this company and the spirits of the
martyred dead seen in Chapter 6:9-11.
There, when these spirits cry for vengeance,
the answer comes to them

"That they should rest yet for a little season, until
their fellow-servants also and their brethren, that
should be killed as they were, should be fulfilled."
This company seems clearly to be the "fellow-servants and brethren" of the spirit martyrs in chapter 6, and have, in the great
tribulation been "killed as they were" and
have "fulfilled" their testimony and life-work
for God by the seal of martyrdom, even as
the waiting ones in chapter six had done in
the centuries which preceded. Thus out from
this great tribulation will come a great host
of martyrs in line with the teaching of chapter 13 concerning the beast who had power to

"Cause that as many as would not worship the
image of the beast should be killed" (13:15).

* * * *

The first company is seen on earth; the second, in heaven.

The whole scene here where we meet the 144,000 is an earthly one. The angels in verse one hold the winds that they should not blow upon "the earth." The judgments of verse 3 fall upon "the earth," and as the company is sealed against these they must be upon the earth when they fall. So too in chapter 14:1 the 144,000 are seen standing with the Lamb upon Mount Sion, on the earth. The generation who lived when Christ came the first time passed from the dispensation of the Old Testament into that of the New, right here upon the earth. So the kingdom of Christ over the Jews will be an earthly kingdom. And this first company evidently passes right here upon earth from this present age into the Millennial Age which shall succeed it. On the other hand

The second company is seen in heaven.

They are declared to be "before the throne of God" in verses 9 and 15. God Himself comforts and the Lamb feeds them (v. 17). He that sitteth on the throne dwells among them (v. 15).

* * * *

The first company comes through the tribulation; the second comes out of it (v. 14).

The 144,000 are seen, as before stated, upon the earth after the tribulation is ended.

Therefore they must have "escaped" it in the sense that they came through it unscathed. This is evidently true of many at that perilous time. For in Matt. 24 Christ warns the Jews to flee to the mountains when the tribulation breaks, evidently for the purpose of escaping its perils . And in verse 22 He says that the days of the tribulation are "shortened" for this very object of saving men, all of whom would otherwise perish. So too in Rev. 12, verses 6 and 14, the picture of the mystical woman shows her, the representative of many, as escaping the power of Satan by fleeing into the wilderness just as Christ had exhorted the Jews to flee to the mountains. Plainly then there are those who pass through the tribulation and come forth from it in safety, and this first company is such.

The second company consists of those *"which came out of great tribulation."* Seen in heaven as they are, they must have come up out of the great tribulation, either from the midst of it, or at its close. They are generally identified as the "tribulation saints," or those who have suffered martyrdom during that time.

The Two Witnesses

(Chapter 11)

God never leaves Himself without witnesses. In all times and crises He has them at hand. So in the Tribulation time God raises up two great, Spirit-filled men who witness for Him with mighty power in those days of spiritual apostasy, and wickedness. Let us note some of the inspired teaching concerning them—First,

* * * *

Their place and time in the story-thread is clear.

When their wonderful resurrection and rapture into heaven is accomplished we read (v. 14)

"The second woe (sixth trumpet) is past; and behold the third woe (seventh trumpet) cometh quickly."

That is their resurrection completes the sixth trumpet, and the seventh immediately follows. This makes their time-position in the narrative perfectly plain. In diagram, as before, it would be as follows—

The Trumpet-Judgments 1 2 3 4 5 6 7

|

The Two Witnesses

Thus their witness ends with the close of the Sixth Trumpet. As it lasts for three and a half years (v. 3) it manifestly begins that far back of this point at which they are resurrected.

* * * *

Their identity is not revealed.

Most expositors believe them to be Moses and Elijah. They base their suggestion upon the description of the witnesses in verse 6 of the chapter. Shutting the heaven that it rain not; turning waters to blood; and smiting the earth with plagues suggests a striking identity with the work of Moses and Elijah when upon earth. Added to this is the clear promise in the last chapter of Malachi (v. 5)—

"Behold I will send you Elijah the prophet before the coming of the great and dreadful day of the Lord."

The evidence seems strong in support of this identification of the witnesses. Yet it is not proof positive. And some suggest that God would more likely raise up His chosen witnesses from men already upon the earth, than bring down from heaven to die, Elijah who had been translated, and Moses who had already suffered death upon the earth.

Let us note some of the striking facts concerning these two witnesses—

* * * *

They are filled with the Spirit of God.

"These are the two olive trees standing before the God of the earth" (v. 4).

The olive tree with its secret flow of oil is the symbol of the Holy Spirit. These two witnesses are pictured as like "two olive trees standing before the God of the earth." That is, through them God pours forth a stream of mighty power by His Spirit. It is the same old secret for us all, this one of spiritual power. The message at the beginning of the age was "ye shall receive power when the Holy Ghost is come upon you." The message at the end of the age for these witnesses is the same. And so is it for us. The earth pours its stream of mystic life through the olive tree while it abides in it. So will God pour forth the stream of His Spirit through us who live in secret touch with Him.

* * * *

They pour forth the Light of God.

For they are also called (v. 4)

"The two candlesticks standing before the God of the earth."

And we know what this light of God is. It is His own Word. With mighty power of the Spirit they pour forth that Word of God which is the message of all His true witnesses. Recall too that they bear this witness of Spirit and Word in the holy city, Jerusalem itself, as verse 8 clearly shows. When we remember that it is in the temple at Jerusalem that the Anti-Christ is manifested, and that in this same city the Two Witnesses bear their testimony we have a remarkable situation indeed. Imagine the

rage of that Anti-Christ as he pours forth
his stream of lies and deceit to the multitudes
who throng the temple courts to do him worship, when in the same city and possibly in
the same temple these two witnesses of God
pour forth their stream of truth in denial
of his word of falsehood and blasphemy. And
as we picture their words of warning and
admonition to the people we can well
imagine one striking feature of that witness.
That is this. *It will be a witness founded on
this Book of Revelation we are now studying.*
For it is God's beacon-light for the age-end.
It will illumine the darkness of those days as
nothing else. Without doubt these candle-
stick-witnesses will pour forth its beams far
and wide upon all who come within their
range. They will warn the people who crowd
the temple of the Man of Sin whom they
come to worship. They will admonish them
of the shortness of his time of triumph; of
the coming of Jesus to destroy him; of the
perils which the tribulation will bring; of
the need of counting not their lives dear unto
themselves when the test of life and death
shall come; of their need to fear not him who
can kill the body only but to fear Him who
can cast both body and soul into hell; of the
splendor and nearness of the King and His
kingdom after they have suffered awhile; of
the sureness that if they suffer with Him
they shall reign with Him; and of the eternal

peace, righteousness, and glory that shall be theirs who endure unto the end even though it may mean martyrdom in the great hour of trial through which they are passing. Mighty indeed will be their testimony from this Book and many believe it is through their witness that the hundred and forty and four thousand of the Jewish tribulation company are brought to Jesus Christ. And note too that—

* * * *

They are Kept by the Power of God.

As they testify they are safeguarded by the miraculous power of God. The man who essays to hurt them or stay their testimony is devoured by fiery flames (v. 5). No man dares to touch them, not even the Man of Sin. Great as his wrath against them must be he cannot lay a hand upon them. They are kept by God's own power. To us comes the same sweet message of God's keeping, in the Spirit's word through Peter (1 Pet. 1:5). *"Kept by the power of God* through faith."* The same power of God which sends the sun blazing across the heavens; the same power which reared on high the sky-piercing mountains; the same power which holds the universe in His mighty hand; the same power which swings this ponderous earth like a toy ball—that power of God is keeping us His children as we walk in the place of witnessing and service where He has placed our

lives. We are immortal till our work is done,
is a blessed truth for all His children who
walk in Him, as well as for these faithful
witnesses who shall so wondrously realize
this truth in the days of the age-end.

* * * *

*Their death seems a failure of God; their
resurrection is the triumph of God.*

To cast the wheat-grains into the entomb-
ing earth and see them go down into darkness and death that *seems* to be failure. To
see nature stripped of her summer beauty
and glory, and robed in garments of death
while winter blasts roar their fierce dirge,
that *seems* to be failure. To see these bodies
in which our loved ones tabernacled here
among us go down to meet corruption; to
hear the awful words "earth to earth, ashes
to ashes, dust to dust," as they fall upon our
bruised and broken hearts like the clods that
fall upon the casket below; that *seems* like
appalling failure. *But God's triumph is al-
ways in resurrection.* It was so with these
two wonderful witnesses of His. It shall be
so at the end of the age in which we live. Let
us not be deceived. There shall be seeming
failure. The foundations will be shaken.
And men will cry out that God has failed.
They cried that when the Lord of glory died
upon a cross. The reason was the same then
as it is now and will be in days to come.
They forgot the resurrection! And if we, the

children of God, are tempted to grow dis-
couraged by the seeming failure of God in
what we see about us in these sobering days
we will do well to remember that the tran-
scendent victory-moment of all time is that
moment when out from the midst of world-
failure and world-disaster a great *Voice,*
the resurrection and rapture voice, calls out
to us from the blue sky behind which He has
hidden Himself,

"COME UP HITHER!"

The Two Wonders

(Chapter 12)

Chapter twelve is another inset. Its imagery is strange and striking. A mystical woman appears in the heavens. She is clothed with the sun. The moon and stars are under her feet. A great red Dragon stands ready to devour the man-child to which she is about to give birth. Who is the woman? What is the story here? What does the symbolism of the chapter stand for?

* * * *

The Dragon is Satan.

"And the great dragon was cast out, that old serpent called the Devil, and Satan" (v. 9).

A good method of approach to so difficult a chapter as this is to find some clear, simple fact and use that as a key to unlock the more difficult parts of the passage. Such is the case here. The identity of the dragon is absolutely clear. The Word leaves no shadow of doubt. It declares him to be "that old serpent, the Devil, and Satan." Hence we build upon a sure foundation when we start with the fact that the dragon is Satan. And this fact becomes a well-nigh irresistible proof of another fact, namely, that

*   *   *   *

The Man-Child is Christ.

The chapter does not explicitly so state. But let us examine the strong circumstantial proof to that effect—

a. It was Christ whom Satan sought to destroy at his birth (v. 4). The second chapter of Matthew makes this plain. In the foreground indeed is Herod. But in the background is Satan. Herod is the human tool but Satan was the real assassin. In Herod's subtle attempt to use the wise-men to betray the place and existence of the young Christ; in the angel's warning to Joseph that Herod was seeking to destroy the young child; and in Herod's cruel edict slaughtering Bethlehem's little ones that he might be sure to compass the death of the Christ-child, we see the details of the death-plot. In all these we see Herod. But Satan as surely used Herod to seek the life of Christ at birth, as he did Judas Iscariot to accomplish His death at the end. All this perfectly parallels the scene in this Revelation picture of the Dragon seeking to devour the Man-Child of the Woman.

b. It was Christ who was "caught up to the throne of God" (v. 5). Of none else could this be said. Others have indeed been caught up into heaven. Both Enoch and Elijah have known that experience. But Jesus Christ is the only one who has been caught up to God's throne. He alone sits at the right hand of the Father on that throne, waiting till His enemies be made His foot-stool. It was He (Acts 7:56) **whom Stephen saw standing at the right hand of God.** This fact of itself would seem almost sufficient to establish that the Man-Child must be Christ. Again—

c. It is Christ who is to "rule all the nations with a rod of iron" (v. 5). Still stronger does this remarkable statement make the chain of evidence in favor of Christ. Who is ever to rule the nations "with a rod of iron" save Himself? Of whom else is this ever said in the Word of God? The psalmist (Ps. 2:9), in speaking of God's gift to His Son of the earth and the nations of it, says:

"Thou shalt break them with a rod of iron."

And in this very book we are now studying (Rev. 19:15), in the sublime picture of the coming of Christ as King, it is said distinctly concerning His relation to the nations:

"And he shall rule them with a rod of iron."

These details then concerning the Man-Child, viz., that he was persecuted at birth by Satan; that he was caught up to the throne of God; and that he shall rule the nations with a rod of iron—seem to be so perfectly fulfilled by Christ and by Him alone that it is difficult to avoid the conclusion that the Man-Child is our Lord Jesus Christ. Out of this rises the natural inference then that

*   *   *   *

The woman clothed with the sun is Israel.

Some think the woman typifies the Holy Spirit. But the woman is the mother of the Man-Child, whom we have seen to be Christ. And the Holy Spirit is never called the mother of Christ. Others see in the woman a type of the Church. But neither is the Church the mother of Christ. She is called the bride of Christ, but never the mother of Christ. She springs from Christ, not Christ from her. On the other hand Christ was born of Israel, after the flesh. He was a true Israelite; the son of David, and the future King of His people. Hence Israel would seem to clearly fulfil the details of this picture of the mystical woman, and the weight of evidence seems to favor this identification.

*   *   *   *

The chapter shows Israel's persecution by Satan and preservation by God.

First Satan seeks through Herod to destroy the Christ at His birth but fails. Then he apparently succeeds in destroying Him on Calvary. But resurrection snatches Him from Satan's grasp and He ascends to the throne of the Father. Then the scene shifts across the great gap of the intervening centuries, to the coming age-end, when Israel shall go through the "great tribulation" pictured by Christ in Matthew 24. Israel is represented as fleeing into the wilderness even as Christ warns them in Matthew to "flee to the mountains." And as Satan persecutes, God preserves His godly remnant of the nation. Twelve hundred and sixty days of verse 6 mark the period of the tribulation, persecution, and correspond to the forty-two months of the power of the Anti-Christ (Rev. 13:5), who heads this time of trouble against Israel. The fleeing to the wilderness and the deliverance by God are real events however difficult may be the interpretation of the symbolism of the eagle wings, the flood of waters, and the opening earth which swallows up the latter. These will all be plain enough when fulfilled. That they stand for realities of deliverance one cannot doubt any more than doubt the divided sea, or the Israel preserved in the wilderness of old. It is the same miracle-working God, saving His own, in both cases.

* * * *

The scene also pictures the next stage in the downfall of Satan.

Not much is said in Scripture about the first step in the fall of that great spirit of evil, Satan. But evidently he was not cast forth entirely from heaven. For in Job (1:6) we see him appearing before God. So too in this chapter he appears to accuse the saints before God in heaven. And we are told that our battling is against principalities and powers "in heavenly places." But here we see the second stage of his downfall, in that he is cast out into *the earth* (v. 9). His wrath is fierce and the tribulation which follows is manifestly the manifestation of it. After the advent of Christ follows the third stage of Satan's fall. He is cast into *the bottomless pit* for a thousand years, the period of the millennium (Rev. 20:1-3). At the close of the thousand years he is "loosed for a little season" (Rev. 20:7). Then his nature is proven unchanged. He goes at his old trade of deceiving men (Rev. 20:8). Then comes the final and eternal stage of his downfall. He is cast forever into *the lake of fire,* arch companion and fellow criminal with the Beast and the false prophet who are already seen there before him (Rev. 20:10).

The Two Beasts

(Revelation 13)

This inset is a biographical sketch of two of the most sinister figures of the book. They are the Two Beasts of Revelation. They are called so because "beast" is the only word to describe their ferocious wickedness and spirit of ravage. The first is a false god. The second his false prophet. Let us study them.

*　*　*　*

The First Beast

He is seemingly the Anti-Christ.

Views differ here. Some regard the second beast (v. 11) as such. Yet the whole picture seems to point to this first beast as the Anti-Christ. Note, for example, that he so preeminently outranks the second beast that he is called in Rev. 20:10 *"The* Beast." Nor does the fact that he combines both civil and ecclesiastical power argue against his being the Anti-Christ. For if he is, as is the case, the perfect imitation and antithesis of Jesus Christ he would need to have this dual character since our Lord Jesus is to be both temporal and spiritual head of the earth when He comes to reign.

*   *   *   *

He is the second person of the Trinity
of Evil.

Attention has often been called to the
striking fact that these two Beasts, with
Satan, constitute a trinity of evil even as the
Father, Son and Holy Spirit constitute the
trinity of the Godhead. God, a Spirit, is
unseen of men, so He manifested Himself in
the flesh through Christ the incarnate Son.
So Satan, a spirit of evil, incarnates himself
in the Beast, who represents him to the
world, and is the Anti-Christ. So too as the
Holy Spirit testifies of, and takes of the
things of Christ, the False Prophet bears
testimony concerning the Beast to the world.
This too seems an incidental proof that this
Beast is the Anti-Christ. For the order of
this trinity of evil, namely, Satan, the Beast,
and the False Prophet, as set over against
God, Christ, and the Spirit, would seem to
make the first Beast the natural antithesis
of Christ even as God is the opposite of
Satan, and the Spirit of Truth the opposite
of the Prophet of Falsehood.

*   *   *   *

He is stamped with the marks and the
power of Satan.

The picture of Satan, the dragon, in Chapter 12:3, and that of the Beast in Chapter
13:1, is an identical one. The symbolism of
both is that of a beast with seven heads and

ten horns, standing for kingdoms and kings. What does this identity signify? Simply that Satan sets up on the earth a vicegerent and representative in the Anti-Christ stamped with his own identity. Christ said "He that hath seen me hath seen the Father." So he who sees the Anti-Christ will see the fleshly incarnation and image of Satan, who works his wicked will through his representative just as the Father carried out His blessed will through His Son. Then too Christ said of Himself, "All power is given unto me in heaven and in earth." So here we are told of the beast (13:2) "the dragon gave him his power, and his seat and great authority." He is the Satan-energized "Man of Sin" even as Christ was the Spirit-empowered Son of God.

* * * *

He is the World-King.

These seven heads of the beast evidently represent seven kingdoms. Daniel's great composite image pictures four of these as the Babylonian, Medo-Persian, Grecian, and Roman empires. Some scholars suggest Egypt, and Assyria as the other two. The seventh and last is that of the Beast or Anti-Christ as here seen. One of these heads was "wounded to death; and his deadly wound was healed." Plainly the significance of this is that one of these kingdoms has been overthrown and will be again revived, as the final world-kingdom of the beast. Many think this to indicate that the last great empire of these six to be overthrown, namely, Rome, will be revived at the age-end and be the form which the kingdom of the Anti-Christ will take. Charlemagne tried world-empire and failed. Napoleon tried, and also failed. The Kaiser has just tried and ended in dismal failure. But the superman of Sin will succeed. For not only does all the symbolism here and in the prophets indicate his kingship of the world, but this chapter sets before us clearly and explicitly the statement (13:7)—

"And power was given him over all kindreds and tongues, and nations."

* * * *

He is the world's god.

"The god of this world" is what the Spirit calls Satan, through Paul. So here the representative whom Satan sets up is the world's false god. Paul pictures him in 1 Thess. 2:4, etc.—

"Who opposeth and exalteth himself above all that is called God, or that is worshipped; so that he *as God* sitteth in the temple of God, showing himself that he is God.'

He exalts himself not only above the true God but above all that is called God. He opposes God. He shows himself as God. He sits in the temple at Jerusalem. There where the Shekinah glory had revealed the presence of the true God this false god manifests forth his own hideous and sinister presence.

And the world worships him! The statement is as clear as it is sobering (13:3-4):

"All the world wondereth after the beast and *they worshipped* the beast."

He is a blasphemer and a braggart (v. 5); he makes war with the saints; his power continues three and a half years (v. 5) another seeming imitation of Christ in the length of his earthly ministry; he delegates power to the false prophet (v. 12) even as Satan had done to him. It is a striking fact that the life and death test of fealty to him is that of the worship of a great image of himself which is set up on earth by his worshipers (v. 14). One cannot miss here the striking parallelism between this last world-king and Nebuchadnezzar, the first world-king with his same life-searching test of a great image to be worshipped under threat of martyrdom to him who refused.

* * * *

He is the world's trade-monopolist.

"No man might buy or sell save he that had the mark" (13:17).

The greed of gain is one of the world's maddest passions. All too well does Satan know this. So another mighty factor is added to the power of the Anti-Christ. He is made the commercial monopolist of the world. A mark is stamped upon the hand or forehead of men. No man can buy or sell without it. Thus a starvation boycott is placed upon all who do not submit to the false-god and his wickedness. No more powerful weapon could be devised. Doubtless it is the climax which forces "all that dwell upon the earth to worship him, whose names are not written in the book of life of the Lamb slain from the foundation of the world" (v. 8). Thank God for the glorious exception! Even in those sinister days God will have His own whom no form of death can swerve from their loyalty to their coming King in order to worship His counterfeit whom that coming shall destroy.

* * * *

His identity is not revealed.

"The mark, or the name of the beast, or the number of his name" (v. 17).

There are three sign-marks of his identity. This verse seventeen discloses them. They are his mark; his name; his mystical number.

His mark is likely his commercial mark, as indicated above. It is the token of his great boycott. It is like a modern business man's trade-mark. Its identity is not here disclosed.

His name also is unrevealed. Many have tried to identify it. Some have seen him in the papacy. Others identify him with Napoleon; others, later, with the Kaiser. But all these are futile conjectures. His scriptural names are well-known. He is the Lawless

One; the Man of Sin; the Son of Perdition. But the name he gives himself and by which he shall be known to the world is plainly not now revealed. Yet it seems clear that it will be when he himself comes. For the fact that this name is written in the hand and forehead of all his worshipers shows that it will then be a matter of world-wide knowledge and understanding.

His mystical number is not yet understood. Doubtless it will be when he comes. But now it is a riddle, a puzzle, a mask to hide his real self. Its trio of sixes is the human, world number in triplicate. It shows him to be indeed a superman. But its tantalizing failure to reach the perfect number of seven, the number of deity, shows his ever-destined failure to reach the height of godhead to which his fierce ambition aspires.

* * * *

He is destroyed by the glory of Christ's appearing.

"Whom the Lord shall destroy with the brightness of His coming."

His fate is a tragedy of judgment. He is destroyed by the blinding glory of Christ's own coming. But here, as elsewhere, destruction, with God, is not annihilation. For he is seen later (19:20) cast "alive" into the lake of fire which becomes his eternal place of punishment. The verb used here for destroy means "to bring to naught," "to make of no effect." The hissing, blazing lightning from mid-heaven withers its victims to helplessness. So the mere presence of Christ in His unspeakable glory palsies the power and person of the beast. The same glory that transforms the believer consumes the wicked. And the face we long to see is the face from which the terrified worldling begs the rocks and hills to hide him (6:16):

*   *   *   *

The Second Beast.

"And I beheld another beast coming up out of the earth" (13:11).

The second beast is the mere tool of the first. As the first is set over against Christ the second is the antithesis of the Holy Spirit. As the Spirit seals men with the seal of God this beast seals them with the mark of the Anti-Christ. The Holy Spirit is the "Spirit of Truth," the second beast is the spirit of deception, even deceiving men with false miracles. As the Holy Spirit leads men to the worship of God and His Christ the second beast compels them to worship the Anti-Christ and his image. As the Spirit is the life-begetter the beast is the life-destroyer. He shares the same fate as the first beast in that his final destiny is also the lake of fire (19:20).

IV.

THE ADVENT

FINAL CHAPTER OUTLINE

The Story-Thread	Chaps.	Insets
INTRODUCTION	1-5	
THE SEALS	6	
	7	The Two Companies
THE TRUMPETS	8-11	
	11	The Two Witnesses
	12	The Two Wonders
	13	The Two Beasts
	14	The First-Fruits, etc.
THE VIALS	15-16	
	17-18	Babylon
THE ADVENT	19	
THE MILLENNIUM	20	
THE NEW HEAVEN AND NEW EARTH	21-22	

The Advent

"Behold, He cometh!" (Rev. 1:7)

The exclamation is a striking one. The Greek word "behold" means "See, look!" It is used to quickly call attention to some striking spectacle which suddenly breaks upon the gaze. As though one should say of some great sight appearing in the heavens before all eyes—"Behold, the comet! Behold, the meteor!" So here. Suddenly, in mid-heaven, without a second's warning, is staged by God the most stupendous sight upon which human eyes have ever gazed,—the outflashing, dazzling, awful splendor of the personal coming of the Lord Jesus Christ in His glory. The earth beholds, and thrills with the first ecstatic moment of her deliverance from the bondage of corruption into the glorious liberty of the sons of God. The angels behold and cry, "The kingdoms of this world are become the kindoms of the Lord and His Christ." The kings and princes of the world behold and cry to the rocks and hills to fall upon them and hide them from His presence. The Anti-Christ beholds and falls palsied and helpless before the breath of His mouth and the glory of His coming. The nations of the earth behold and "wail because of His coming." "BEHOLD!" For not since the skies were stretched by the omnipotent hand of God in the ages that are past has their blue canopy been the setting for such a scene as now floods them with its glory. Let us study the picture as the Scripture word-paints it (Chap. 19:11-21):

11 And I saw heaven opened, and behold a white horse; and he that sat upon him was called Faithful and True, and in righteousness he doth judge and make war.

12 His eyes were as a flame of fire, and on his head were many crowns; and he had a name written, that no man knew, but he himself.

13 And he was clothed with a vesture dipped in blood: and his name is called The Word of God.

14 And the armies which were in heaven followed him upon white horses, clothed in fine linen, white and clean.

15 And out of his mouth goeth a sharp sword, that with it he should smite the nations: and he shall rule them with a rod of iron: and he treadeth the winepress of the fierceness and wrath of Almighty God.

16 And he hath on his vesture and on his thigh a name written, KING OF KINGS, AND LORD OF LORDS.

*　*　*　*

He comes to judge individual sin. God hates sin. It is the tragedy of His universe. Let none think it will escape His wrath. For all these centuries His wrath against sin has been biding its time. Its day of reckoning is coming. He could not be a just God and fail to judge that which has brought such wreck and ruin to His own fair creation. And that wrath falls at the coming of His Son. He is its swift and unerring minister. "He treadeth the winepress of the fierceness and wrath of Almighty God" (v. 15). Sin cannot escape those eyes which are as a flame of fire. "Wherever the carcass is there will the vultures be" when He comes. That is, wherever the corruption of sin is found there will His keen-eyed ministers of wrath visit His judgment upon it. No sin can be so hidden or secret but it will be searched out and judged by the scorching flames of His wrath when He shall come again.

He comes to judge national sin (v. 15). Not only does He judge sin in the individual. But He has also a score to settle with nations as such. It is the nations He smites with His sword (v. 15). It is the nations He is to "rule with a rod of iron." It is the nations who array themselves against Him (v. 19) on the side of the Beast, when He comes in His glory. It is the nations who are judged by Him in the scene of the gathering of the sheep and the goats in Matt. 25. Tyranny, oppression, cruelty, drunkenness, idolatry, and many kindred national sins must be judged by Him, and nations are called to an account of their stewardship when He shall come to judge the world.

He comes to judge the Man of Sin. The world's individual sin and national sin climax in a Man of Sin. He is the devil's masterpiece, even as Christ was the express image of God. All the hideousness, blackness, and brazen effrontery of sin are embodied in him. The world which rejected the Christ receives and enthrones the Anti-Christ (13: 8). In him sin unmasks itself and usurps the very throne which Christ has come to take. The man of Sin becomes the outstanding figure of a world which God means shall be ruled by His own Righteous One. Therefore the Christ who came to judge sin cannot miss sin's most shining mark. The Holy One can brook no such rival as the Sinful One. Swiftly and terribly does His judgment fall upon the arch-usurper of His own Kingdom. Blasted by the "breath of His mouth" and blinded by "the brightness of His coming" (2 Thes. 2:8) the Beast whom Christ's coming finds arrayed at the head of the nations against Him (19:19) is "taken" and meets his final and irretrievable doom in the lake of fire "prepared for the devil and his angels."

* * * *

After the Advent

The Binding of Satan. With individual and national sin judged, and the Man of Sin overcome, the next event is the binding of Satan. For Jesus Christ is about to enter upon His kingdom, and before He does so it is the will of God that Satan, His arch-enemy, should be fettered for all the duration of

that kingdom. So John sees a mighty angel
come down from heaven and bind Satan
with a great chain for the thousand years of
Christ's reign upon earth (20:1-3). Some
take exception to the thought of binding a
mighty spirit of evil with "a chain." But
there need be no quibble here. For God has
other chains than those of steel or brass. The
earth, for example, is bound to the sun by
a mighty chain of attraction which is both
immaterial and invisible. Yet no man can
break its power. So here God uses metaphors
which our finite minds can grasp. And we
may be assured that no human nor demon
power can break the unseen fetters by which
God binds the imprisoned spirit of wickedness during the golden age of Christ's rulership upon earth. And that brings us naturally to the next great fact, viz.,

The Millennial Reign of Jesus Christ. "The
Son of Man is like unto a man who has gone
into a far country to receive for himself a
kingdom and to return." These words of
the Master exactly describe His absence from
the earth now. He has gone to the Father
to receive for Himself His kingdom. When
He returns it will be to set up this kingdom.
This is the great event which now takes place
after the binding of Satan. John sees the
martyred dead (20:4) and the distinct statement is made that being resurrected "they
reigned with Christ a thousand years." The

word "millennium" means literally "a thousand years." It is here explicitly stated that Christ reigns for that period upon the earth. Five times in the first seven verses of the chapter is this period of a thousand years mentioned. This of itself is sufficient answer to the objection that this is the only place in the Word the Millennium is mentioned. But there are scores of prophecies in both Old Testament and New which predict the reign of Jesus Christ upon the earth when He shall come again. Here at the beginning of the millennium we see it inaugurated. All the prophets tell of its glory and blessedness. The earth shall be delivered from the bondage of physical corruption (Rom. 8:21); the wilderness shall blossom as the rose; the desert shall become a place of fountains and refreshing streams; the power of sin and death shall be restrained; the glory of the Lord shall cover the earth as the waters cover the seas; the banishment of the savage nature from the wild beasts and the beautiful picture of a little child leading them shall have its real and literal fulfilment; the government shall be upon His shoulders and of the increase of righteousness and peace there shall be no end. It is then that Paul's word is fulfilled that 'the saints shall judge the earth" and our Lord's promise also that they which overcome shall sit down with Him upon His throne even as He is seated upon the Father's throne.

The Revolt of the Nations (20:7-10). The statement (19:15) that Christ shall during this period rule the nations "with a rod of iron" while it indicates universal subjugation evidently does not teach universal conversion. And that the unregenerate human heart is ever the same is shown by the fact that when Satan is "loosed for a little season" at the close of the Millennium (vs. 3 and 7) the nations revolt against the Lord Christ and are judged for the same (v. 9). At this same time Satan meets his final doom and is cast at the end of the Millennium, into the same lake of fire which had engulfed the Beast and the False Prophet at its beginning (v. 10).

The Great White Throne Judgment (20: 11-15). When the righteous dead are raised and enter upon their reign with Jesus Christ (20:4) we are told (v. 5) that " the rest of the dead lived not again until the thousand years were finished." Here then in verse 12 at the close of the thousand years we see "the rest of the dead" raised and judged before the great white throne. This is what is known as the judgment of the wicked dead. All here are condemned who are not found written in the book of life. At the same time Death, Christ's last enemy, and Hell are both destroyed. That is Death, which takes the bodies, and Hades, which takes the spirits, of the lost, both cease to exist being swallowed up in the lake of fire which is henceforth the final place of doom for Satan and those who have rejected Jesus Christ.

The New Heaven and New Earth (Chaps. 21-22). After this judgment John sees the new heaven and new earth. God's great purpose of love and grace now reaches its climax. Heaven and earth are practically united. The tabernacle of God is with men and He dwells with them. All tears are forever wiped away. Death has vanished. Sorrow and pain cease. Life flows from the throne of God as a great river. The curse is banished. Night has fled away. His servants commune with Him face to face and do His will in blessed and joyous service. The Church, as the Bride of Christ, is seen descending from heaven under the similitude of a great city. It needs no sun, for the glory of God lightens it and the Lamb is the light thereof. Destiny is fixed for he who is filthy is called upon to remain such, while he who is righteous is also to be righteous still. The great book closes with a solemn warning against those who add to or take away from its precious message; a repetition of our Lord's blessed promise that He will come quickly; and the responsive thrill of the heart and cry of the lips from the enraptured prisoner upon lonely Patmos

"EVEN SO COME, LORD JESUS!"

www.bookjungle.com *email: sales@bookjungle.com fax: 630-214-0564 mail: Book Jungle PO Box 2226 Champaign, IL 61825*

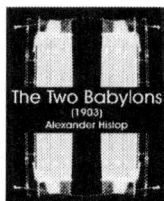

The Two Babylons
Alexander Hislop

You may be surprised to learn that many traditions of Roman Catholicism in fact don't come from Christ's teachings but from an ancient Babylonian "Mystery" religion that was centered on Nimrod, his wife Semiramis, and a child Tammuz. This book shows how this ancient religion transformed itself as it incorporated Christ into its teachings....

Religion/History   Pages:353

ISBN: *1-59462-010-5*   *MSRP* **$22.95**

QTY

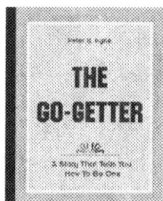

The Go-Getter
Kyne B. Peter

The Go Getter is the story of William Peck.He was a war veteran and amputee who will not be refused what he wants. Peck not only fights to find employment but continually proves himself more than competent at the many difficult test that are throw his way in the course of his early days with the Ricks Lumber Company...

Business/Self Help/Inspirational   Pages:68

ISBN: *1-59462-186-1*   *MSRP* **$8.95**

QTY

The Power Of Concentration
Theron Q. Dumont

It is of the utmost value to learn how to concentrate. To make the greatest success of anything you must be able to concentrate your entire thought upon the idea you are working on. The person that is able to concentrate utilizes all constructive thoughts and shuts out all destructive ones..

Self Help/Inspirational   Pages:196

ISBN: *1-59462-141-1*   *MSRP* **$14.95**

Self Mastery
Emile Coue

Emile Coue came up with novel way to improve the lives of people. He was a pharmacist by trade and often saw ailing people. This lead him to develop autosuggestion, a form of self-hypnosis. At the time his theories weren't popular but over the years evidence is mounting that he was indeed right all along...

New Age/Self Help   Pages:98

ISBN: *1-59462-189-6*   *MSRP* **$7.95**

Rightly Dividing The Word
Clarence Larkin

The "Fundamental Doctrines" of the Christian Faith are clearly outlined in numerous books on Theology, but they are not available to the average reader and were mainly written for students. The Author has made it the work of his ministry to preach the "Fundamental Doctrines." To this end he has aimed to express them in the simplest and clearest manner..

Religion   Pages:352

ISBN: *1-59462-334-1*   *MSRP* **$23.45**

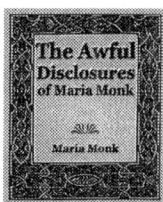

The Awful Disclosures Of
Maria Monk

"I cannot banish the scenes and characters of this book from my memory. To me it can never appear like an amusing fable, or lose its interest and importance. The story is one which is continually before me, and must return fresh to my mind with painful emotions as long as I live..."

Religion   Pages:232

ISBN: *1-59462-160-8*   *MSRP* **$17.95**

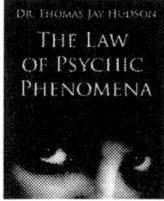

The Law of Psychic Phenomena
Thomson Jay Hudson

"I do not expect this book to stand upon its literary merits; for if it is unsound in principle, felicity of diction cannot save it, and if sound, homeliness of expression cannot destroy it. My primary object in offering it to the public is to assist in bringing Psychology within the domain of the exact sciences. That this has never been accomplished..."

New Age   Pages:420

ISBN: *1-59462-124-1*   *MSRP* **$29.95**

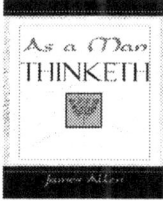

As a Man Thinketh
James Allen

"This little volume (the result of meditation and experience) is not intended as an exhaustive treatise on the much-written-upon subject of the power of thought. It is suggestive rather than explanatory, its object being to stimulate men and women to the discovery and perception of the truth that by virtue of the thoughts which they choose and encourage..."

Inspirational/Self Help   Pages:80

ISBN: *1-59462-231-0*   *MSRP* **$9.45**

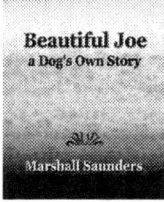

Beautiful Joe
Marshall Saunders

When Marshall visited the Moore family in 1892, she discovered Joe, a dog they had nursed back to health from his previous abusive home to live a happy life. So moved was she, that she wrote this classic masterpiece which won accolades and was recognized as a heartwarming symbol for humane animal treatment...

Fiction   Pages:256

ISBN: *1-59462-261-2*   *MSRP* **$18.45**

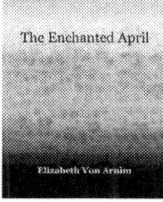

The Enchanted April
Elizabeth Von Arnim

It began in a woman's club in London on a February afternoon, an uncomfortable club, and a miserable afternoon when Mrs. Wilkins, who had come down from Hampstead to shop and had lunched at her club, took up The Times from the table in the smoking-room...

Fiction   Pages:368

ISBN: *1-59462-150-0*   *MSRP* **$23.45**

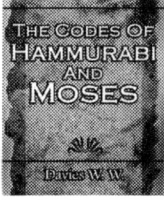

The Codes Of Hammurabi And
Moses - W. W. Davies

The discovery of the Hammurabi Code is one of the greatest achievements of archaeology, and is of paramount interest, not only to the student of the Bible, but also to all those interested in ancient history...

Religion   Pages:132

ISBN: *1-59462-338-4*   *MSRP* **$12.95**

Holland - The History Of Netherlands
Thomas Colley Grattan

Thomas Grattan was a prestigious writer from Dublin who served as British Consul to the US. Among his works is an authoritative look at the history of Holland. A colorful and interesting look at history....

History/Politics   Pages:408

ISBN: *1-59462-137-3*   *MSRP* **$26.95**

The Thirty-Six Dramatic Situations
Georges Polti

An incredibly useful guide for aspiring authors and playwrights. This volume categorizes every dramatic situation which could occur in a story and describes them in a list of 36 situations. A great aid to help inspire or formalize the creative writing process...

Self Help/Reference   Pages:204

ISBN: *1-59462-134-9*   *MSRP* **$15.95**

A Concise Dictionary of Middle English
A. L. Mayhew
Walter W. Skeat

The present work is intended to meet, in some measure, the requirements of those who wish to make some study of Middle-English, and who find a difficulty in obtaining such assistance as will enable them to find out the meanings and etymologies of the words most essential to their purpose...

Reference/History   Pages:332

ISBN: *1-59462-119-5*   *MSRP* **$29.95**

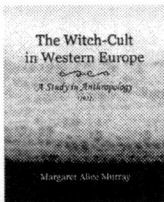

The Witch-Cult in Western Europe
Margaret Murray
QTY

The mass of existing material on this subject is so great that I have not attempted to make a survey of the whole of European "Witchcraft" but have confined myself to an intensive study of the cult in Great Britain. In order, however, to obtain a clearer understanding of the ritual and beliefs I have had recourse to French and Flemish sources...

Occult   Pages:308
ISBN: 1-59462-126-8   MSRP $22.45

The Science Of Psychic Healing
Yogi Ramacharaka

This book is not a book of theories it deals with facts. Its author regards the best of theories as but working hypotheses to be used only until better ones present themselves. The "fact" is the principal thing the essential thing to uncover which the tool, theory, is used...

New Age/Health   Pages:180
ISBN: 1-59462-140-3   MSRP $13.95

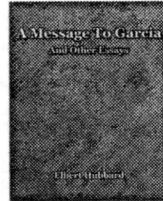

Bible Myths
Thomas Doane

In pursuing the study of the Bible Myths, facts pertaining thereto, in a condensed form, seemed to be greatly needed, and nowhere to be found. Widely scattered through hundreds of ancient and modern volumes, most of the contents of this book may indeed be found; but any previous attempt to trace exclusively the myths and legends...

Religion/History   Pages:644
ISBN: 1-59462-163-2   MSRP $38.95

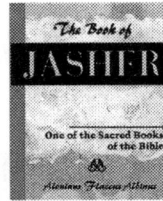

Tertium Organum
P. D. Ouspensky

A truly mind expanding writing that combines science with mysticism with unprecedented elegance. He presents the world we live in as a multi dimensional world and time as a motion through this world. But this isn't a cold and purely analytical explanation but a masterful presentation filled with similes and analogies...

New Age   Pages:356
ISBN: 1-59462-205-1   MSRP $23.95

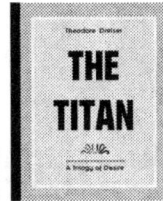

Advance Course in Yogi Philosophy
Yogi Ramacharaka

"The twelve lessons forming this volume were originally issued in the shape of monthly lessons, known as "The Advanced Course in Yogi Philosophy and Oriental Occultism" during a period of twelve months beginning with October, 1904, and ending September, 1905."

Philosophy/Inspirational/Self Help   Pages:340
ISBN: 1-59462-229-9   MSRP $22.95

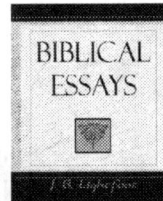

Ambassador Morgenthau's Story
Henry Morgenthau

"By this time the American people have probably become convinced that the Germans deliberately planned the conquest of the world. Yet they hesitate to convict on circumstantial evidence and for this reason all eye witnesses to this, the greatest crime in modern history, should volunteer their testimony..."

History   Pages:472
ISBN: 1-59462-244-2   MSRP $29.95

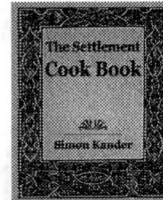

The Aquarian Gospel of Jesus the Christ
Levi Dowling

A retelling of Jesus' story which tells us what happened during the twenty year gap left by the Bible's New Testament. It tells of his travels to the far-east where he studied with the masters and fought against the rigid caste system. This book has enjoyed a resurgence in modern America and provides spiritual insight with charm. Its influences can be seen throughout the Age of Aquarius.

Religion   Pages:264
ISBN: 1-59462-321-X   MSRP $18.95

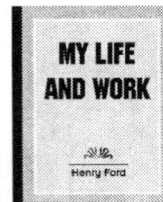

Philosophy Of Natural Therapeutics
Henry Lindlahr
QTY

We invite the earnest cooperation in this great work of all those who have awakened to the necessity for more rational living and for radical reform in healing methods...

Health/Philosophy/Self Help   Pages:552
ISBN: 1-59462-132-2   MSRP $34.95

A Message to Garcia
Elbert Hubbard

This literary trifle, A Message to Garcia, was written one evening after supper, in a single hour. It was on the Twenty-second of February, Eighteen Hundred Ninety-nine, Washington's Birthday, and we were just going to press with the March Philistine...

New Age/Fiction   Pages:92
ISBN: 1-59462-144-6   MSRP $9.95

The Book of Jasher
Alcuinus Flaccus Albinus

The Book of Jasher is an historical religious volume that many consider as a missing holy book from the Old Testament. Particularly studied by the Church of Later Day Saints and historians, it covers the history of the world from creation until the period of Judges in Israel. It's authenticity is bolstered due to a reference to the Book of Jasher in the Bible in Joshua 10:13

Religion/History   Pages:276
ISBN: 1-59462-197-7   MSRP $18.95

The Titan
Theodore Dreiser

"When Frank Algernon Cowperwood emerged from the Eastern District Penitentiary, in Philadelphia he realized that the old life he had lived in that city since boyhood was ended. His youth was gone, and with it had been lost the great business prospects of his earlier manhood. He must begin again..."

Fiction   Pages:564
ISBN: 1-59462-220-5   MSRP $33.95

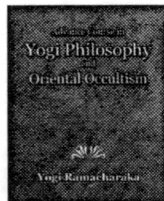

Biblical Essays
J. B. Lightfoot

About one-third of the present volume has already seen the light. The opening essay "On the Internal Evidence for the Authenticity and Genuineness of St John's Gospel" was published in the "Expositor" in the early months of 1890, and has been reprinted since...

Religion/History   Pages:480
ISBN: 1-59462-238-8   MSRP $30.95

The Settlement Cook Book
Simon Kander

A legacy from the civil war, this book is a classic "American charity cookbook," which was used for fundraisers starting in Milwaukee. While it has transformed over the years, this printing provides great recipes from American history. Over two million copies have been sold. This volume contains a rich collection of recipes from noted chefs and hostesses of the turn of the century...

How-to   Pages:472
ISBN: 1-59462-256-6   MSRP $29.95

My Life and Work
Henry Ford

Henry Ford revolutionized the world with his implementation of mass production for the Model T automobile. Gain valuable business insight into his life and work with his own auto-biography... "We have only started on our development of our country we have not as yet, with all our talk of wonderful progress, done more than scratch the surface. The progress has been wonderful enough but..."

Biographies/History/Business   Pages:300
ISBN: 1-59462-198-5   MSRP $21.95

QTY

The Rosicrucian Cosmo-Conception Mystic Christianity by *Max Heindel* ISBN: *1-59462-188-8* **$38.95**
The Rosicrucian Cosmo-conception is not dogmatic, neither does it appeal to any other authority than the reason of the student. It is not controversial, but is set forth in the, hope that it will help to clear... New Age/Religion Pages 646

Abandonment To Divine Providence by *Jean-Pierre de Caussade* ISBN: *1-59462-228-0* **$25.95**
"The Rev. Jean Pierre de Caussade was one of the most remarkable spiritual writers of the Society of Jesus in France in the 18th Century. His death took place at Toulouse in 1751. His works have gone through many editions and have been republished... Inspirational/Religion Pages 400

Mental Chemistry by *Charles Haanel* ISBN: *1-59462-192-6* **$23.95**
Mental Chemistry allows the change of material conditions by combining and appropriately utilizing the power of the mind. Much like applied chemistry creates something new and unique out of careful combinations of chemicals the mastery of mental chemistry... New Age Pages 354

The Letters of Robert Browning and Elizabeth Barret Barrett 1845-1846 vol II ISBN: *1-59462-193-4* **$35.95**
by *Robert Browning* and *Elizabeth Barrett* Biographies Pages 596

Gleanings In Genesis (volume I) by *Arthur V. Pink* ISBN: *1-59462-130-6* **$27.45**
Appropriately has Genesis been termed "the seed plot of the Bible" for in it we have, in germ form, almost all of the great doctrines which are afterwards fully developed in the books of Scripture which follow... Religion Inspirational Pages 420

The Master Key by *L. W. de Laurence* ISBN: *1-59462-001-6* **$30.95**
In no branch of human knowledge has there been a more lively increase of the spirit of research during the past few years than in the study of Psychology, Concentration and Mental Discipline. The requests for authentic lessons in Thought Control, Mental Discipline and... New Age/Business Pages 422

The Lesser Key Of Solomon Goetia by *L. W. de Laurence* ISBN: *1-59462-092-X* **$5.95**
This translation of the first book of the "Lernegton" which is now for the first time made accessible to students of Talismanic Magic was done, after careful collation and edition, from numerous Ancient Manuscripts in Hebrew, Latin, and French... New Age/Occult Pages 92

Rubaiyat Of Omar Khayyam by *Edward Fitzgerald* ISBN:*1-59462-332-5* **$13.95**
Edward Fitzgerald, whom the world has already learned, in spite of his own efforts to remain within the shadow of anonymity, to look upon as one of the rarest poets of the century, was born at Bredfield, in Suffolk, on the 31st of March, 1809. He was the third son of John Purcell... Music Pages 172

Ancient Law by *Henry Maine* ISBN: *1-59462-128-4* **$29.95**
The chief object of the following pages is to indicate some of the earliest ideas of mankind, as they are reflected in Ancient Law, and to point out the relation of those ideas to modern thought. Religion/History Pages 452

Far-Away Stories by *William J. Locke* ISBN: *1-59462-129-2* **$19.45**
"Good wine needs no bush, but a collection of mixed vintages does. And this book is just such a collection. Some of the stories I do not want to remain buried for ever in the museum files of dead magazine-numbers an author's not unpardonable vanity..." Fiction Pages 272

Life of David Crockett by *David Crockett* ISBN: *1-59462-250-7* **$27.45**
"Colonel David Crockett was one of the most remarkable men of the times in which he lived. Born in humble life, but gifted with a strong will, an indomitable courage, and unremitting perseverance... Biographies/New Age Pages 424

Lip-Reading by *Edward Nitchie* ISBN: *1-59462-206-X* **$25.95**
Edward B. Nitchie, founder of the New York School for the Hard of Hearing, now the Nitchie School of Lip-Reading, Inc, wrote "LIP-READING Principles and Practice". The development and perfecting of this meritorious work on lip-reading was an undertaking... How-to Pages 400

A Handbook of Suggestive Therapeutics, Applied Hypnotism, Psychic Science ISBN: *1-59462-214-0* **$24.95**
by *Henry Munro* Health/New Age Health/Self-help Pages 376

A Doll's House: and Two Other Plays by *Henrik Ibsen* ISBN: *1-59462-112-8* **$19.95**
Henrik Ibsen created this classic when in revolutionary 1848 Rome. Introducing some striking concepts in playwriting for the realist genre, this play has been studied the world over. Fiction/Classics/Plays 308

The Light of Asia by *sir Edwin Arnold* ISBN: *1-59462-204-3* **$13.95**
In this poetic masterpiece, Edwin Arnold describes the life and teachings of Buddha. The man who was to become known as Buddha to the world was born as Prince Gautama of India but he rejected the worldly riches and abandoned the reigns of power when... Religion/History Biographies Pages 170

The Complete Works of Guy de Maupassant by *Guy de Maupassant* ISBN: *1-59462-157-8* **$16.95**
"For days and days, nights and nights, I had dreamed of that first kiss which was to consecrate our engagement, and I knew not on what spot I should put my lips..." Fiction/Classics Pages 240

The Art of Cross-Examination by *Francis L. Wellman* ISBN: *1-59462-309-0* **$26.95**
Written by a renowned trial lawyer, Wellman imparts his experience and uses case studies to explain how to use psychology to extract desired information through questioning. How-to/Science/Reference Pages 408

Answered or Unanswered? by *Louisa Vaughan* ISBN: *1-59462-248-5* **$10.95**
Miracles of Faith in China Religion Pages 112

The Edinburgh Lectures on Mental Science (1909) by *Thomas* ISBN: *1-59462-008-3* **$11.95**
This book contains the substance of a course of lectures recently given by the writer in the Queen Street Hall, Edinburgh. Its purpose is to indicate the Natural Principles governing the relation between Mental Action and Material Conditions... New Age/Psychology Pages 148

Ayesha by *H. Rider Haggard* ISBN: *1-59462-301-5* **$24.95**
Verily and indeed it is the unexpected that happens! Probably if there was one person upon the earth from whom the Editor of this, and of a certain previous history, did not expect to hear again... Classics Pages 380

Ayala's Angel by *Anthony Trollope* ISBN: *1-59462-352-X* **$29.95**
The two girls were both pretty, but Lucy who was twenty-one who supposed to be simple and comparatively unattractive, whereas Ayala was credited as her Bombwhat romantic name might show, with poetic charm and a taste for romance. Ayala when her father died was nineteen... Fiction Pages 484

The American Commonwealth by *James Bryce* ISBN: *1-59462-286-8* **$34.45**
An interpretation of American democratic political theory. It examines political mechanics and society from the perspective of Scotsman James Bryce Politics Pages 572

Stories of the Pilgrims by *Margaret P. Pumphrey* ISBN: *1-59462-116-0* **$17.95**
This book explores pilgrims religious oppression in England as well as their escape to Holland and eventual crossing to America on the Mayflower, and their early days in New England... History Pages 268

BOOK JUNGLE

Bringing Classics to Life

www.bookjungle.com *email: sales@bookjungle.com fax: 630-214-0564 mail: Book Jungle PO Box 2226 Champaign, IL 61825*

QTY

The Fasting Cure *by Sinclair Upton*   ISBN: *1-59462-222-1* **$13.95**
In the Cosmopolitan Magazine for May, 1910, and in the Contemporary Review (London) for April, 1910, I published an article dealing with my experiences in fasting. I have written a great many magazine articles, but never one which attracted so much attention... New Age/Self Help/Health Pages 164

Hebrew Astrology *by Sepharial*   ISBN: *1-59462-308-2* **$13.45**
In these days of advanced thinking it is a matter of common observation that we have left many of the old landmarks behind and that we are now pressing forward to greater heights and to a wider horizon than that which represented the mind-content of our progenitors... Astrology Pages 144

Thought Vibration or The Law of Attraction in the Thought World   ISBN: *1-59462-127-6* **$12.95**
by William Walker Atkinson   *Psychology/Religion Pages 144*

Optimism *by Helen Keller*   ISBN: *1-59462-108-X* **$15.95**
Helen Keller was blind, deaf, and mute since 19 months old, yet famously learned how to overcome these handicaps, communicate with the world, and spread her lectures promoting optimism. An inspiring read for everyone... Biographies/Inspirational Pages 84

Sara Crewe *by Frances Burnett*   ISBN: *1-59462-360-0* **$9.45**
In the first place, Miss Minchin lived in London. Her home was a large, dull, tall one, in a large, dull square, where all the houses were alike, and all the sparrows were alike, and where all the door-knockers made the same heavy sound... Childrens/Classic Pages 88

The Autobiography of Benjamin Franklin *by Benjamin Franklin*   ISBN: *1-59462-135-7* **$24.95**
The Autobiography of Benjamin Franklin has probably been more extensively read than any other American historical work, and no other book of its kind has had such ups and downs of fortune. Franklin lived for many years in England, where he was agent... Biographies/History Pages 332

Name	
Email	
Telephone	
Address	
City, State ZIP	

☐ **Credit Card**   ☐ **Check / Money Order**

Credit Card Number	
Expiration Date	
Signature	

Please Mail to: Book Jungle
PO Box 2226
Champaign, IL 61825
or Fax to: 630-214-0564

ORDERING INFORMATION

web: *www.bookjungle.com*
email: *sales@bookjungle.com*
fax: *630-214-0564*
mail: *Book Jungle PO Box 2226 Champaign, IL 61825*
or PayPal *to sales@bookjungle.com*

Please contact us for bulk discounts

DIRECT-ORDER TERMS

20% Discount if You Order Two or More Books
Free Domestic Shipping!
Accepted: Master Card, Visa, Discover, American Express

www.ingramcontent.com/pod-product-compliance
Lightning Source LLC
LaVergne TN
LVHW081324060426

835511LV00011B/1851